HTML, CSS & JavaScript All-in-One

Mastering Front-End Development

THOMPSON CARTER

TABLE OF CONTENTS

INTRODUCTION

HTML, CSS & JavaScript All-in-One: Mastering Front-End Development"

The web development landscape is constantly evolving, and with it, the demand for skilled front-end developers who can create responsive, interactive, and visually appealing websites. Front-end development, the art of building what users see and interact with on the web, is foundational to the entire web experience. From the basic structure of a webpage to the complex, dynamic interactions on modern sites, mastering front-end technologies such as HTML, CSS, and JavaScript is essential for anyone looking to build a career in web development.

This book, "HTML, CSS & JavaScript All-in-One: Mastering Front-End Development," is designed to guide you through the core technologies of front-end web development, with a focus on practical applications, clear explanations, and real-world examples. Whether you are a complete beginner or an experienced developer looking to deepen your skills, this book provides a structured approach to learning that covers everything from the fundamentals to advanced concepts. By the end, you'll not only understand how each technology works independently, but you'll also have the skills to combine them to build full-fledged, modern websites.

The Importance of Front-End Development

Front-end development is the bridge between the user and the information or services that a website provides. A website's front-end encompasses everything that a user interacts with — the layout, the buttons, the images, the text, and even the dynamic features like form validation, navigation menus, and real-time data updates.

In the past, web design was primarily about creating static pages with a few basic features. But today, front-end development has evolved into a complex and multifaceted field. Websites and web applications are now expected to be fast, responsive, interactive, and capable of running across a wide variety of devices and screen sizes. This shift has led to the development of a powerful suite of technologies—**HTML**, **CSS**, and **JavaScript**—that, when used together, allow developers to create rich user experiences.

What You Will Learn

This book is organized into 20 chapters that cover every aspect of front-end development. From the basics of HTML to the intricacies of JavaScript programming, you will gain a comprehensive understanding of the skills required to succeed as a front-end developer.

- **HTML (Hypertext Markup Language)**: You will learn how to structure web pages using semantic HTML, which provides the foundation for creating content on the web. HTML is essential for creating the skeleton of a webpage, allowing you to define headings, paragraphs, lists, links, forms, and more.

- **CSS (Cascading Style Sheets)**: After mastering HTML, you'll learn how to style your content with CSS. You'll understand how to control layout, fonts, colors, and spacing, as well as how to use advanced techniques like Flexbox, Grid, and media queries to make your website responsive and visually appealing on any device.
- **JavaScript**: With JavaScript, you'll learn how to add interactivity to your websites. JavaScript lets you manipulate the DOM (Document Object Model), handle events like clicks and key presses, fetch data from APIs, and create dynamic web applications that can react to user input in real-time.

Additionally, the book introduces you to key front-end development concepts like responsive design, mobile-first strategies, debugging, version control with Git, modern development tools and frameworks, performance optimization, and web accessibility.

Real-World Approach to Learning

Each chapter is filled with **real-world examples** and **practical exercises** to ensure that you're not just reading about these technologies but actually using them to build projects. Throughout the book, you will work through examples ranging from a simple static webpage to more complex dynamic sites, including a fully functional portfolio website by the end of the book. This project-based learning approach ensures that you gain hands-on experience with each concept, reinforcing your understanding as you apply what you've learned.

The examples provided are not just theoretical. They reflect the common challenges and situations you'll face as a front-end developer working on real-world projects. Whether it's creating a responsive design for a mobile device or implementing form validation with JavaScript, these examples are designed to give you the skills and confidence to tackle similar problems in your own projects.

Why HTML, CSS, and JavaScript Are Essential

- **HTML** is the backbone of any webpage. Without HTML, web browsers wouldn't know how to display text, images, links, and other elements. HTML defines the content and structure of a page, allowing developers to organize and present information in a meaningful way.
- **CSS** is the visual face of a website. It controls how the elements defined in HTML are styled and positioned on the page. Without CSS, websites would be plain, unstyled, and difficult to navigate. CSS enables developers to create visually appealing, responsive, and user-friendly designs that work across various devices and screen sizes.

- **JavaScript** brings web pages to life by adding interactivity and dynamic behavior. From simple form validation to complex animations and real-time data updates, JavaScript enables developers to build rich, user-friendly experiences that go beyond static content. With JavaScript, you can make web pages interactive, responsive, and capable of reacting to user input in real-time.

Together, HTML, CSS, and JavaScript form the core of front-end development, and a strong understanding of these technologies is crucial for building modern websites and web applications. This book will help you master each of these technologies and integrate them into full-fledged projects.

Who This Book is For

This book is designed for a wide range of readers:

- **Beginners**: If you are new to web development, this book will walk you through the fundamentals, providing you with a solid foundation in HTML, CSS, and JavaScript.
- **Intermediate Developers**: If you have some experience with front-end development but need a deeper understanding of certain concepts, this book will provide more advanced techniques and best practices.
- **Anyone Interested in Web Development**: Whether you are a designer looking to transition into front-end

development or a back-end developer wanting to learn the front-end, this book will provide you with the skills you need.

What You Can Expect

As you progress through the book, you'll encounter a series of progressively challenging projects and exercises that help solidify your learning. Each chapter is structured with clear explanations, code snippets, and practical examples that provide you with both the theoretical background and the practical know-how to implement the concepts.

By the end of this book, you will have a deep understanding of front-end development and be capable of building dynamic, responsive websites and web applications. You'll also be equipped with the tools and knowledge to continue learning and staying up to date with the latest trends and technologies in web development.

In the following chapters, you'll learn how to create the building blocks of the web and transform simple static pages into fully interactive, modern websites. Let's get started!

CHAPTER 1: INTRODUCTION TO FRONT-END DEVELOPMENT

Overview of Front-End Development

Front-end development refers to the part of web development that involves creating the user-facing side of a website or application. It's the interface that users interact with directly — everything from buttons and navigation menus to images and videos. This part of development is crucial because it determines the user experience (UX), which significantly affects how users engage with a product.

At its core, front-end development involves three primary technologies:

1. **HTML (HyperText Markup Language)**: The structure of a webpage.
2. **CSS (Cascading Style Sheets)**: The styling (look and feel) of the webpage.
3. **JavaScript (JS)**: The interactivity of the webpage, making it dynamic and responsive.

While these three technologies form the backbone of front-end development, the landscape has evolved significantly with the advent of frameworks, libraries, and tools that make building complex, interactive websites easier and more efficient. Some of the popular tools and frameworks include:

- **React**, **Vue**, and **Angular** for building dynamic user interfaces.
- **Sass** and **LESS** for advanced CSS capabilities.
- **Webpack**, **Babel**, and **npm** for managing assets and dependencies.

Front-end developers work closely with **back-end developers** who handle the server-side of applications — things like databases, APIs, and business logic. The front-end and back-end interact via **APIs (Application Programming Interfaces)**, allowing data and information to flow between the two. For example, when a user submits a form on a website, the front-end sends the data to the back-end, which processes the request and sends back a response.

In essence, **front-end development is the bridge between user needs and technical systems**. A well-designed front end ensures that users can easily navigate, interact with, and derive value from a web application, while a poor front end can make even the most advanced application feel unintuitive and cumbersome.

Roles and Tools in Front-End Development

To build effective and efficient front-end websites, developers use various **tools** and **environments**. Below are some key elements that every front-end developer should be familiar with:

1. **Integrated Development Environments (IDEs) and Text Editors**
   - **VS Code**: A popular, lightweight IDE for web development, known for its rich extensions, syntax highlighting, and debugging features.
   - **Sublime Text** and **Atom**: Other text editors often favored for their speed and simplicity.
   - **WebStorm**: An IDE tailored for JavaScript development, with powerful refactoring tools and deep integration with popular JS frameworks.

   These tools help streamline coding, testing, and debugging by providing syntax highlighting, auto-completion, and error identification, making it easier for developers to focus on writing high-quality code.

2. **Version Control: Git and GitHub**
   - **Git** is a version control system that tracks changes to code over time, allowing developers to collaborate efficiently, manage different versions of a project, and roll back changes when needed.

- o **GitHub** (or GitLab, Bitbucket, etc.) provides cloud-based repositories to store code, collaborate with teams, and manage project versions. It's vital for maintaining code history and supporting team collaboration in front-end development.
- o **Basic Git Commands**:
  - git init: Initializes a new Git repository.
  - git clone: Clones an existing repository.
  - git add: Adds changes to the staging area.
  - git commit: Saves changes to the local repository.
  - git push: Pushes changes to the remote repository (e.g., GitHub).
  - git pull: Pulls the latest changes from the remote repository.

With these tools, developers can manage and track their codebase as well as collaborate with other developers by working on different branches and merging changes seamlessly.

3. **Package Managers and Task Runners**
   - o **npm** (Node Package Manager) is used for managing JavaScript libraries and dependencies. You can install libraries like React, Lodash, and

Axios to simplify tasks like DOM manipulation or making HTTP requests.

o **Yarn** is an alternative to npm with faster performance and better dependency management.

o **Webpack**, **Parcel**, and **Gulp** are tools for automating tasks like bundling JavaScript files, processing CSS, and optimizing images.

Real-World Example: How Front-End Code Creates a Modern Website Layout

Let's imagine you're tasked with building a simple portfolio website. Here's how front-end code would structure it:

1. **HTML**: The foundational structure of the website — headings, paragraphs, images, links, and navigation. This content is defined using HTML tags.

   o For example, you might define the header with <header>, the navigation menu with <nav>, and the main content with <main>.

html

```
<header>
  <h1>My Portfolio</h1>
  <nav>
    <ul>
```

```
      <li><a href="#about">About</a></li>
      <li><a href="#projects">Projects</a></li>
      <li><a href="#contact">Contact</a></li>
    </ul>
  </nav>
</header>
```

2. **CSS**: Styling the page — fonts, colors, spacing, and layout. Here, CSS defines the look and feel, turning the raw HTML into something visually appealing.

   o For instance, CSS would center your navigation links, choose a color scheme, and set the layout for mobile responsiveness.

css

```
body {
    font-family: Arial, sans-serif;
    background-color: #f4f4f4;
}

header {
    background-color: #333;
    color: #fff;
    padding: 20px;
    text-align: center;
}

nav ul {
```

```
    list-style-type: none;
    padding: 0;
}

nav ul li {
    display: inline;
    margin-right: 20px;
}
```

3. **JavaScript**: Interactivity — for example, when a user clicks a button to reveal a hidden section or submit a form. JavaScript is used to enhance the user experience.

   o For example, clicking a "Load More" button might reveal additional projects or information.

javascript

```
const loadMoreButton = document.querySelector('#load-more');
loadMoreButton.addEventListener('click', function() {
    alert('More content will be loaded!');
});
```

This simple example demonstrates how HTML, CSS, and JavaScript work together to create the structure, appearance, and interactivity of a modern webpage.

Getting Started: Setting Up Your First Project and Understanding the Workflow

To begin your journey into front-end development, you'll need to set up a basic project. Here's a step-by-step guide to get started:

1. **Setting Up the Project Structure**

   o Create a folder for your project, e.g., portfolio-project.

   o Inside that folder, create three files:

     ▪ index.html — your HTML file.

     ▪ styles.css — your CSS file.

     ▪ script.js — your JavaScript file.

2. **Editing the Files**

   o Open your files in a text editor like **VS Code**.

   o Start by adding some basic HTML to your index.html file, linking to your CSS and JavaScript files.

html

```html
<html lang="en">
<head>
  <meta charset="UTF-8">
  <meta name="viewport" content="width=device-width, initial-scale=1.0">
  <title>My Portfolio</title>
  <link rel="stylesheet" href="styles.css">
</head>
<body>
  <h1>Welcome to My Portfolio</h1>
  <script src="script.js"></script>
</body>
```

```
</html>
```

3. **Opening Your Project in a Browser**

   o   Save all the files and open index.html in your browser
       to see the result. This is where you'll view your web
       page as you develop it.

4. **Using Git for Version Control**

   o   Initialize a Git repository in your project folder
       using git init.

   o   Create your first commit: git add . and git commit -m
       "Initial commit".

   o   If using GitHub, create a remote repository and
       push your code using git push origin master.

5. **Experimenting and Iterating**

   o   Modify your HTML, CSS, and JavaScript as you go.
       Refresh your browser to see the changes in real time.

   o   Use Git to track changes and manage different
       versions of your project.

By the end of this chapter, you'll have a fundamental
understanding of front-end development, including the key roles,
tools, and workflow. You'll also be able to set up your first front-
end project, write HTML and CSS, and enhance it with basic
JavaScript functionality.

CHAPTER 2: THE BUILDING BLOCKS OF THE WEB – HTML

What is HTML?

HTML, or **HyperText Markup Language**, is the foundational language of the web. It is used to structure content on the web by marking up text, images, links, and other media. HTML documents are composed of a series of **tags** that tell the web browser how to display content.

At its core, HTML serves as the **skeleton** of a webpage. It outlines the structure of a webpage using a set of predefined tags. These tags group content into headings, paragraphs, lists, and links, helping both the browser and users understand the relationship between different pieces of information.

Every HTML document starts with a simple structure that includes the following components:

1. **DOCTYPE Declaration**: Tells the browser which version of HTML is being used.
2. **HTML Tags**: Encloses all the content of the document.

3. **Head Section**: Contains meta-information, such as title, character encoding, and links to external resources like CSS files.

4. **Body Section**: Contains the actual content of the webpage, such as text, images, links, and other media.

html

```
<!DOCTYPE html>
<html lang="en">
<head>
  <meta charset="UTF-8">
  <meta name="viewport" content="width=device-width, initial-scale=1.0">
  <title>My Webpage</title>
</head>
<body>
  <h1>Welcome to My Webpage</h1>
  <p>This is my first webpage using HTML!</p>
</body>
</html>
```

In this example, the <!DOCTYPE html> declaration at the top defines the document type, ensuring that the browser correctly interprets it as HTML5. The <html> tag surrounds the entire content, the <head> tag holds the meta information, and the <body> tag holds the visible content.

Essential HTML Tags

HTML uses a set of **tags** to define the structure and elements of a webpage. Each tag generally has an opening tag and a closing tag. The closing tag includes a forward slash (/) before the tag name. Here are some of the most essential HTML tags:

1. **<html>**: This is the root tag that contains all the HTML elements.
   o Example: <html lang="en"> defines the language of the document as English.
2. **<head>**: Contains meta-information about the document, such as title, character encoding, and links to external resources (like stylesheets and scripts).
   o Example: <meta charset="UTF-8"> specifies the character encoding.
3. **<body>**: This tag contains the actual content of the webpage that users see.
   o Example: <body> will contain all the visible elements, such as text, images, and links.
4. **<div>**: A container element that is used for grouping content together. It has no inherent style or meaning but is useful for structuring a page.
   o Example: <div class="container"> could be used to group all content within a specific section of a page.
5. **<p>**: Represents a paragraph of text.
   o Example: <p>This is a paragraph.</p> defines a block of text.

6. **<a>**: Creates a hyperlink, allowing users to navigate from one page to another.

    o Example: <a href="https://www.example.com">Click here</a> creates a link that points to another webpage.

7. **<img>**: Embeds an image in the document.

    o Example: <img src="image.jpg" alt="A descriptive text of the image"> embeds an image with a description for accessibility.

8. **<ul>, <ol>, <li>**: These tags are used to create lists. <ul> creates an unordered list (bulleted), <ol> creates an ordered list (numbered), and <li> defines list items.

    o Example (Unordered List):

    html

    ```
    <ul>
      <li>Item 1</li>
      <li>Item 2</li>
    </ul>
    ```

Semantic HTML

In HTML, **semantic tags** refer to elements that convey meaning about the content they enclose. These tags are more meaningful and descriptive than generic tags like <div> and <span>. They help improve accessibility, SEO (Search Engine Optimization), and overall code clarity.

1. **\<header\>**: Represents the header of a page or a section, typically containing navigation links or introductory content.

    o Example:

    html

    ```
    <header>
      <h1>Welcome to My Website</h1>
      <nav>
        <ul>
          <li><a href="#home">Home</a></li>
          <li><a href="#about">About</a></li>
        </ul>
      </nav>
    </header>
    ```

2. **\<footer\>**: Represents the footer of a page or a section, typically containing copyright information, contact details, or other relevant links.

    o Example:

    html

    ```
    <footer>
      <p>&copy; 2024 My Website</p>
    ```

```
</footer>
```

3. **<article>**: Represents a self-contained piece of content, such as a blog post or news article.

   o Example:

   html

   ```
   <article>
     <h2>Understanding HTML</h2>
     <p>HTML is the basic building block of web development...</p>
   </article>
   ```

4. **<section>**: Represents a section of content, typically with its own heading. It's often used to group content related to a specific topic.

   o Example:

   html

   ```
   <section>
     <h2>Features</h2>
     <p>Our website offers amazing features...</p>
   </section>
   ```

5. **<nav>**: Represents a navigation section containing links to other pages or sections of the site.

   o Example:

html

```
<nav>
 <ul>
   <li><a href="#home">Home</a></li>
   <li><a href="#contact">Contact</a></li>
 </ul>
</nav>
```

Using semantic HTML enhances the accessibility of your website for users with disabilities (e.g., screen readers) and makes your code more understandable for other developers. Moreover, it helps search engines better index your content.

Real-World Example: Writing a Simple Webpage Layout with HTML

Let's apply the HTML knowledge you've learned to build a simple webpage layout. We will create a basic structure for a personal website with a header, navigation bar, main content, and footer.

html

```
<!DOCTYPE html>
<html lang="en">
<head>
   <meta charset="UTF-8">
   <meta name="viewport" content="width=device-width, initial-scale=1.0">
   <title>My Personal Website</title>
</head>
```

```
<body>
  <header>
    <h1>Welcome to My Personal Website</h1>
    <nav>
      <ul>
        <li><a href="#about">About Me</a></li>
        <li><a href="#portfolio">Portfolio</a></li>
        <li><a href="#contact">Contact</a></li>
      </ul>
    </nav>
  </header>

  <section id="about">
    <h2>About Me</h2>
    <p>Hello, I'm a web developer passionate about creating beautiful and
functional websites.</p>
  </section>

  <section id="portfolio">
    <h2>My Portfolio</h2>
    <p>Check out some of the projects I've worked on!</p>
    <ul>
      <li>Project 1</li>
      <li>Project 2</li>
      <li>Project 3</li>
    </ul>
  </section>

  <footer>
    <p>&copy; 2024 My Personal Website</p>
```

```
</footer>
</body>
</html>
```

In this example, we've created:

- A **header** with a title and navigation links.
- Two **sections**: one for "About Me" and another for "Portfolio."
- A **footer** with copyright information.

This simple structure uses both **semantic** and **non-semantic** tags to build a basic, easy-to-understand webpage layout.

In this chapter, we've explored **HTML** as the fundamental building block of web development. You learned the essential tags used to structure content on the web, such as headings, paragraphs, lists, links, and images. We also covered the importance of **semantic HTML** and how it contributes to accessibility, SEO, and code clarity.

As you move forward in your front-end development journey, HTML will serve as the foundation upon which you'll build the rest of your webpages, adding styles with CSS and interactivity with JavaScript. In the next chapter, we'll dive deeper into CSS, the language that defines the look and feel of your web pages.

CHAPTER 3: STRUCTURING WEB PAGES WITH HTML

Creating Basic Layouts: Using Containers like <div> and <section>
A fundamental aspect of web development is how content is arranged on the page. HTML provides a variety of tags to organize and group content for readability, structure, and styling. While CSS will be used for positioning and design, HTML gives the page its **structure**.

1. <div>: The Generic Container

The <div> tag is one of the most commonly used elements in HTML. It's a generic container element that has no inherent styling or meaning but is invaluable for grouping content together.

html

```
<div class="container">
    <h1>Welcome to My Website</h1>
    <p>This is a simple webpage layout.</p>
```

```
</div>
```

In this example, the <div> groups the content together. Developers often use <div> with CSS classes or IDs to style the content collectively.

2. <section>: Defining Content Areas

A more semantic way to group content is through the <section> tag. A section represents a thematic grouping of content and is usually associated with a heading. It helps to break down your page into distinct areas that represent different topics.

html

```
<section>
   <h2>About Me</h2>
   <p>I am a web developer passionate about creating clean and accessible websites.</p>
</section>
```

In this example, the <section> helps identify the "About Me" part of the webpage and organizes the content meaningfully.

3. Nesting Containers for Complex Layouts

Often, you'll need to nest these tags to create more complex layouts. By combining <div>, <section>, and other structural tags, you can build flexible, well-organized page layouts.

html

```
<div class="main-content">
  <section class="introduction">
    <h2>Welcome to My Blog</h2>
    <p>Here you can find articles on web development, design, and
technology.</p>
  </section>
  <section class="latest-posts">
    <h2>Latest Posts</h2>
    <article>
      <h3>How to Learn HTML</h3>
      <p>HTML is the foundation of the web...</p>
    </article>
    <article>
      <h3>Getting Started with CSS</h3>
      <p>CSS is used to style and layout web pages...</p>
    </article>
  </section>
</div>
```

In this example, the content is divided into sections like "Introduction" and "Latest Posts" using <section>. These sections are further broken down into individual articles with <article> tags.

Forms and Input Elements

Forms are critical for interacting with users and gathering data. Whether it's a login page, a contact form, or a comment section, forms allow users to submit information to the server. HTML provides various form elements to create forms that collect different types of data.

1. <form>: The Form Tag

The <form> tag is the container that wraps all the form elements. It defines the action that will be taken when the form is submitted (e.g., sending data to the server) and the method (GET or POST).

html

```
<form action="/submit" method="POST">
   <!-- Form elements go here -->
</form>
```

2. Input Elements

The <input> tag is used to collect different types of data. The type attribute defines the kind of input (text, password, checkbox, etc.).

html

```
<label for="name">Name:</label>
<input type="text" id="name" name="name">
```

In this example:

- <label> defines a text label for the input field.
- The for attribute of the label associates it with the id of the <input> field.

Common Input Types:

- type="text": Standard text input.
- type="password": Hides the input text for passwords.
- type="email": Validates email addresses.
- type="submit": Button that submits the form.

3. Buttons

The <button> element is used for creating clickable buttons. It's often used within forms to trigger an action, like submitting data.

html

```
<button type="submit">Submit</button>
```
This button will submit the form when clicked.

4. Textarea

The <textarea> element allows users to enter multiple lines of text, ideal for comments or messages.

html

```
<label for="message">Your Message:</label>
<textarea id="message" name="message" rows="4" cols="50"></textarea>
```
Here, the user can write a message in a larger input box.

Links and Navigation

Navigation is an essential part of any website. HTML provides a simple way to create links (<a>) and organize them into menus (<nav>). These elements allow users to navigate through the pages of your website or external resources.

1. <a>: Creating Links

The <a> (anchor) tag is used to create hyperlinks. The href attribute specifies the URL the link points to.

html

```
<a href="https://www.example.com">Visit Example Website</a>
```
In this example, clicking the link will open the URL specified in the href attribute.

2. Links to Sections within the Same Page

You can also link to specific sections within the same page by using id attributes.

html

```
<a href="#about">Go to About Section</a>
...
<section id="about">
    <h2>About Me</h2>
    <p>This is the about section.</p>
</section>
```

When the link is clicked, the browser will scroll to the section with the corresponding id.

3. <nav>: Defining Navigation Menus

The <nav> tag defines a section of links dedicated to navigation. It helps search engines and assistive technologies recognize the structure of the page.

html

```
<nav>
  <ul>
    <li><a href="#home">Home</a></li>
    <li><a href="#about">About</a></li>
    <li><a href="#services">Services</a></li>
    <li><a href="#contact">Contact</a></li>
  </ul>
</nav>
```

In this example, the <nav> tag wraps an unordered list of navigation links. When users click these links, they are taken to different sections of the webpage.

Real-World Example: Building a Basic Blog Page with HTML Content, Navigation, and a Comment Form

Let's combine everything we've learned so far and create a basic blog page. This example will include a header, navigation menu, content section with articles, and a comment form.

html

```
<!DOCTYPE html>
<html lang="en">
<head>
  <meta charset="UTF-8">
  <meta name="viewport" content="width=device-width, initial-scale=1.0">
  <title>My Blog</title>
</head>
<body>
  <!-- Header with Navigation -->
  <header>
    <h1>Welcome to My Blog</h1>
    <nav>
      <ul>
        <li><a href="#home">Home</a></li>
        <li><a href="#about">About</a></li>
        <li><a href="#contact">Contact</a></li>
      </ul>
    </nav>
  </header>

  <!-- Blog Content -->
  <section id="home">
    <article>
      <h2>How to Learn HTML</h2>
```

```
    <p>HTML is the foundation of web development. In this post, we'll
explore the basics...</p>
    </article>

    <article>
      <h2>Getting Started with CSS</h2>
      <p>CSS allows you to style your HTML documents. Learn the basics of
CSS syntax...</p>
    </article>
  </section>

  <!-- Comment Form -->
  <section id="comments">
    <h2>Leave a Comment</h2>
    <form action="/submit-comment" method="POST">
      <label for="name">Name:</label>
      <input type="text" id="name" name="name" required><br><br>

      <label for="comment">Comment:</label><br>
      <textarea id="comment" name="comment" rows="4" cols="50"
required></textarea><br><br>

      <button type="submit">Submit</button>
    </form>
  </section>

  <!-- Footer -->
  <footer>
    <p>&copy; 2024 My Blog</p>
  </footer>
```

```
</body>
</html>
```

In this example:

- **Navigation**: The header contains a navigation menu linking to different sections of the page.
- **Blog Content**: Two blog posts are displayed within <article> tags, grouped in a <section> with the id="home".
- **Comment Form**: Below the content, a simple form collects the user's name and comment.
- **Footer**: The page ends with a footer that displays the copyright information.

This chapter has introduced the essential techniques for **structuring web pages with HTML**. By utilizing containers like <div> and <section>, you can organize your content in a meaningful way. Forms allow you to collect data from users, and navigation links enable easy movement through your website. The real-world example of a blog page demonstrated how all these elements come together in practice.

In the next chapter, we will dive into **CSS**, which will help bring your HTML structures to life by adding styles and layouts.

CHAPTER 4: INTRODUCTION TO CSS – STYLING THE WEB

What is CSS? – Explaining the Role of CSS in Web Design and Layout

CSS (Cascading Style Sheets) is a stylesheet language used to control the **look and feel** of web pages. While HTML provides the structure and content, CSS defines how that content is presented to the user. This includes visual elements such as colors, fonts, layout, spacing, and positioning.

In simpler terms, HTML is like the **skeleton** of a webpage, and CSS is the **clothing** that makes it look appealing and user-friendly. Through CSS, you can create visually engaging websites by altering various aspects of a page's design.

Key Points:

- **CSS Controls Design**: Fonts, colors, margins, paddings, spacing, and positioning.
- **Separation of Concerns**: By keeping the design (CSS) separate from the content (HTML), websites are easier to maintain and update.
- **Responsive Design**: CSS plays a critical role in making webpages look good on all screen sizes, from desktops to mobile phones.

CSS Syntax and Selectors – Understanding Selectors, Properties, and Values

CSS works by applying **styles** (like fonts, colors, and spacing) to HTML elements. These styles are defined using a **selector**, which targets specific HTML elements, followed by the styles you wish to apply.

1. CSS Syntax:

The basic syntax of a CSS rule consists of three components:

- **Selector**: The HTML element you want to style.
- **Property**: The specific style you want to change (like color, font-size, or margin).
- **Value**: The value of the property you're changing (e.g., a color code or pixel size).

css

```
selector {
   property: value;
}
```

For example:

css

```
h1 {
   color: blue;
   font-size: 36px;
}
```

In this case, the **selector** is h1, meaning all <h1> elements in the HTML document. The **properties** are color and font-size, with values of blue and 36px, respectively.

2. Common CSS Selectors:

- **Element Selector**: Targets all elements of a particular type (e.g., h1, p, div).

  css

  ```
  p {
     font-family: Arial, sans-serif;
  }
  ```

- **Class Selector**: Targets all elements with a specific class attribute. Classes are denoted with a . before the class name.

css

```
.button {
    background-color: green;
    color: white;
}
```

- **ID Selector**: Targets a specific element with a unique id attribute. IDs are denoted with a # before the ID name.

css

```
#header {
    background-color: #333;
    color: white;
}
```

- **Universal Selector**: Selects all elements on the page.

css

```
* {
    margin: 0;
    padding: 0;
}
```

- **Descendant Selector**: Targets elements within another element.

css

```
.container p {
    font-size: 18px;
}
```

Inline, Internal, and External CSS – How to Apply Styles Using Different Methods

There are three main ways to apply CSS to an HTML document: **inline**, **internal**, and **external**.

1. Inline CSS: Inline CSS is used directly within an HTML tag using the style attribute. This method is not ideal for larger projects because it mixes HTML with CSS, making it harder to maintain.

html

```
<h1 style="color: blue; font-size: 36px;">Welcome to My Website</h1>
```

This will apply the styles directly to that specific <h1> element. While convenient for quick tests or small modifications, inline CSS should be avoided in larger projects for maintainability and scalability reasons.

2. Internal CSS: Internal CSS is placed within the <style> tag in the <head> section of the HTML document. This method allows you to define styles for an entire page, but they will only apply to that specific page. It's suitable for smaller websites or pages where external stylesheets aren't needed.

html

```
<head>
  <style>
    body {
      background-color: lightgray;
      font-family: Arial, sans-serif;
    }

    h1 {
      color: green;
    }
  </style>
</head>
```

3. External CSS: External CSS is the most recommended method for large websites because it keeps styles separate from HTML, allowing for better organization and reusability. An external CSS file is linked to the HTML document with the <link> tag.

html

```
<head>
  <link rel="stylesheet" href="styles.css">
</head>
```

In the styles.css file:

css

```
body {
  background-color: lightgray;
```

```
    font-family: Arial, sans-serif;
}

h1 {
    color: green;
}
```

This is the most efficient method for larger projects because you can have one CSS file to style multiple HTML pages.

Real-World Example: Styling a Webpage with Basic Color, Fonts, and Layout Adjustments

Let's create a simple webpage and style it with CSS, adjusting basic properties like color, font, and layout.

HTML Structure:

html

```
<!DOCTYPE html>
<html lang="en">
<head>
    <meta charset="UTF-8">
    <meta name="viewport" content="width=device-width, initial-scale=1.0">
    <title>My Stylish Website</title>
    <link rel="stylesheet" href="styles.css">
</head>
<body>
    <header>
```

```
      <h1>Welcome to My Stylish Website</h1>
   </header>
   <section>
      <h2>About Me</h2>
      <p>This is a simple webpage to demonstrate CSS styling.</p>
   </section>
   <footer>
      <p>Contact us at: contact@stylishwebsite.com</p>
   </footer>
</body>
</html>
```

CSS (styles.css):

css

```css
/* Body and Background */
body {
   background-color: #f4f4f4;
   font-family: 'Arial', sans-serif;
   margin: 0;
   padding: 0;
}

/* Header Style */
header {
   background-color: #4CAF50;
   color: white;
   text-align: center;
   padding: 20px 0;
}
```

```
/* Section Style */
section {
    padding: 20px;
    margin: 20px;
    background-color: white;
    border-radius: 8px;
    box-shadow: 0 4px 8px rgba(0, 0, 0, 0.1);
}


h2 {
    color: #333;
}


/* Footer Style */
footer {
    background-color: #333;
    color: white;
    text-align: center;
    padding: 10px;
    position: fixed;
    bottom: 0;
    width: 100%;
}
```

Explanation of Styling:

- **Body:** The background-color is set to a light gray (#f4f4f4) and the font is set to Arial. We've removed default margins and padding to clean up the page.

- **Header:** A green background (#4CAF50) with white text and centered alignment gives the page a clean header.
- **Section:** The section is given padding for spacing, a white background, rounded corners (border-radius), and a subtle shadow for a card-like appearance.
- **Footer:** The footer is styled similarly to the header but with a dark background (#333) and fixed at the bottom of the page, ensuring it's always visible.

Result: This simple layout results in a stylish, clean webpage with well-spaced sections, readable fonts, and a polished look.

In this chapter, we've introduced **CSS** as the tool to style and design your webpages. You learned about the essential CSS syntax, including selectors, properties, and values. We covered the different ways to apply styles—**inline, internal,** and **external**—with a focus on the best practices for maintainable code. Lastly, you saw a real-world example of how to style a webpage with CSS by adjusting colors, fonts, and layout.

Next, we'll dive deeper into **CSS Layouts** to understand how to control positioning and create complex layouts using **Flexbox** and **CSS Grid**. This will enable you to create responsive and dynamic web pages.

CHAPTER 5: UNDERSTANDING THE CSS BOX MODEL

The Box Model Explained: Margin, Border, Padding, and Content Areas

One of the foundational concepts in CSS is the **box model**. This model defines how elements on a web page are structured and how space is allocated around them. Understanding the box model is crucial because it directly affects how layout and spacing are handled on a webpage.

The box model breaks down an HTML element into four primary components:

1. **Content**: This is the actual content of the element, such as text, images, or other HTML elements. It's the innermost part of the box.

2. **Padding**: Padding is the space between the content and the element's border. It increases the space around the content, but still within the element's box.

3. **Border**: The border surrounds the padding (if any) and the content. It is a line (or area) that wraps the content and padding, which can be customized in terms of thickness, style, and color.

4. **Margin**: Margin is the outermost layer and the space outside the border. It separates an element from others, providing spacing between different elements on the page.

Here's a visual representation of the box model:

lua

```
+-----------------------------+
|         Margin              |
|  +-----------------------+  |
|  |      Border           |  |
|  |  +-----------------+  |  |
|  |  |   Padding       |  |  |
|  |  |+-------------+  |  |  |
|  |  || Content     |  |  |  |
|  |  |+-------------+  |  |  |
|  |  +-----------------+  |  |
```

```
|   +------------------------+  |
+------------------------------+
```

- **Content Area**: Where the actual content (text, images, etc.) resides.
- **Padding**: Space between the content and the border.
- **Border**: The line around the padding.
- **Margin**: Space between the border and surrounding elements.

Setting Width and Height: Working with Box Dimensions

Now that we understand the basic structure of an element, let's talk about **setting dimensions** (width and height) and how they interact with the box model.

1. **Width & Height**: The width and height properties in CSS define the size of the content area. By default, the width and height apply only to the content area, and the padding, border, and margin are added outside of these dimensions.

   Example:

   css

   ```css
   div {
       width: 300px;
       height: 200px;
   ```

```
    background-color: lightblue;
}
```

In this case, the width of the div is 300px, and the height is 200px. However, these dimensions only apply to the content box, and the padding, border, and margin will be added outside of this area.

2. **Box-Sizing Property**: By default, the dimensions of an element (width and height) only apply to the content box. However, by setting box-sizing: border-box;, you can include the padding and border within the width and height.

Example:

css

```
div {
    box-sizing: border-box;
    width: 300px;
    height: 200px;
    padding: 20px;
    border: 5px solid black;
    background-color: lightblue;
}
```

Here, the width and height include the padding and border. So, the total size of the element will still be 300px by 200px, including all the padding and borders.

CSS Display Property: Block vs Inline Elements and How They Affect Layout

The display property in CSS is crucial for determining how an element behaves in the layout. The two most commonly used values for display are block and inline.

1. **Block Elements**: Block elements take up the full width available, and each one starts on a new line, stacking vertically. By default, elements like <div>, <p>, <h1>, and <ul> are block-level elements.

   Block elements:

   - o Start on a new line.
   - o Stretch to fill the entire width of their container (unless a width is specified).
   - o Can have width, height, margin, and padding applied.

   Example:

   css

   ```
   div {
       display: block;
       width: 100%;
       height: 150px;
       background-color: lightblue;
   ```

```
}
```

In this case, the div takes up the full width of its parent container and starts on a new line.

2. **Inline Elements**: Inline elements, such as <span>, <a>, and <strong>, do not start on a new line. They only take up as much width as necessary and allow other elements to sit next to them in the same line.

Inline elements:

- o Do not start on a new line.
- o Take up only as much width as necessary.
- o Cannot have width or height set (unless you change them to inline-block).

Example:

css

```
span {
    display: inline;
    color: red;
}
```

The span element will remain inline with surrounding content and will only take up the space necessary for its text.

3. **Inline-Block Elements**: The inline-block value allows an element to behave like an inline element (staying in the same line) while also allowing it to have width and height applied, like a block element.

Example:

css

```
div {
    display: inline-block;
    width: 100px;
    height: 100px;
    background-color: lightblue;
}
```

The div will behave like an inline element (it won't start on a new line) but will still allow you to set its width and height.

Real-World Example: Styling a Product Grid with Margin, Padding, and Borders

Let's apply everything we've learned so far to a real-world example: creating a simple product grid. This grid will use div elements to represent individual products, and we'll apply margin, padding, and borders to make the layout clean and organized.

HTML:

html

```html
<!DOCTYPE html>
<html lang="en">
<head>
  <meta charset="UTF-8">
  <meta name="viewport" content="width=device-width, initial-scale=1.0">
  <title>Product Grid</title>
  <link rel="stylesheet" href="styles.css">
</head>
<body>
  <div class="product-grid">
    <div class="product">
      <img src="product1.jpg" alt="Product 1">
      <h3>Product 1</h3>
      <p>$29.99</p>
    </div>
    <div class="product">
      <img src="product2.jpg" alt="Product 2">
      <h3>Product 2</h3>
      <p>$19.99</p>
    </div>
    <div class="product">
      <img src="product3.jpg" alt="Product 3">
      <h3>Product 3</h3>
      <p>$39.99</p>
    </div>
    <!-- More products... -->
  </div>
</body>
```

```
</html>
```

CSS (styles.css):

css

```css
/* Body */
body {
    font-family: Arial, sans-serif;
    background-color: #f4f4f4;
    margin: 0;
    padding: 20px;
}


/* Product Grid */
.product-grid {
    display: flex;
    flex-wrap: wrap;
    gap: 20px;
    justify-content: center;
}


/* Individual Product */
.product {
    background-color: white;
    border: 1px solid #ddd;
    border-radius: 8px;
    padding: 20px;
    width: 200px;
    text-align: center;
    box-shadow: 0 4px 8px rgba(0, 0, 0, 0.1);
}
```

```
.product img {
    width: 100%;
    height: auto;
    border-radius: 4px;
}

/* Product Title and Price */
.product h3 {
    margin: 10px 0;
    font-size: 18px;
}

.product p {
    color: #888;
    font-size: 16px;
}
```

Explanation of Styling:

- **.product-grid**: This container uses **Flexbox** to align the products in a row, with wrapping enabled and a gap between the items. The justify-content: center; ensures that the products are centered within the container.

- **.product**: Each product is styled with padding, a border, and a box-shadow to give it a card-like appearance. The border radius (border-radius: 8px) creates rounded corners, and padding: 20px adds space inside each product.

- **.product img**: The images are set to a responsive size, making sure they fill the width of their container but maintain their aspect ratio.
- **Product Title and Price**: The h3 title and p price are styled with margins for spacing and font adjustments for readability.

In this chapter, we learned about the **CSS box model**, one of the most fundamental concepts in web design. Understanding how **content, padding, border,** and **margin** interact is essential for creating well-structured layouts. We also explored the display property and how it affects the layout of elements, from **block** to **inline** and **inline-block**. Finally, we worked on a **real-world example** to practice these concepts, building a simple product grid with margin, padding, borders, and Flexbox.

In the next chapter, we'll dive into more advanced layout techniques with **Flexbox** and **CSS Grid** to help you build more complex, responsive layouts.

CHAPTER 6: LAYOUT TECHNIQUES – FLEXBOX AND GRID

CSS Flexbox: A One-Dimensional Layout Model

Flexbox (Flexible Box Layout) is a CSS layout model designed to arrange items in a one-dimensional space, either in a row or a column. It is incredibly useful for creating responsive designs and aligning elements in a flexible way. Flexbox allows items to adapt and distribute space according to the container's available size, making it a powerful tool for modern web design.

Key Concepts in Flexbox

1. **Flex Container**: The parent element that holds the flex items. It's defined using the display: flex; property.
2. **Flex Items**: The child elements inside the flex container. These are the items that will be arranged or aligned according to the flexbox rules.

Properties of the Flex Container

- display: flex;: This turns the container into a flex container.
- flex-direction: This defines the direction in which the flex items are laid out. It can be row (default), column, row-reverse, or column-reverse.
- justify-content: This aligns the items along the main axis (horizontal in a row, vertical in a column).
  - flex-start, flex-end, center, space-between, space-around, and space-evenly.
- align-items: This aligns the items along the cross-axis (perpendicular to the main axis).
  - flex-start, flex-end, center, baseline, and stretch.
- align-self: Allows individual items to override the align-items property and align themselves differently.

- flex-wrap: This controls whether the items should wrap onto the next line when there is not enough space. Values: nowrap (default), wrap, wrap-reverse.

Properties of Flex Items

- flex-grow: Defines the ability for a flex item to grow if there is extra space available. The default is 0 (no growth).
- flex-shrink: Defines the ability for a flex item to shrink if there is not enough space. The default is 1 (it shrinks).
- flex-basis: Defines the initial size of a flex item before it starts to grow or shrink.
- flex: A shorthand for flex-grow, flex-shrink, and flex-basis combined. For example, flex: 1 is the same as flex-grow: 1; flex-shrink: 1; flex-basis: 0;.
- align-self: Aligns an individual item within its container, overriding the container's align-items.

Example: Basic Flexbox Layout

Let's build a simple layout using Flexbox to create a row of items that adjust their spacing dynamically.

html

```
<!DOCTYPE html>
<html lang="en">
<head>
  <meta charset="UTF-8">
```

```
<meta name="viewport" content="width=device-width, initial-scale=1.0">
<title>Flexbox Layout Example</title>
<style>
    .flex-container {
        display: flex;
        justify-content: space-between;
        align-items: center;
        height: 100vh;
        background-color: #f0f0f0;
        padding: 20px;
    }
    .flex-item {
        background-color: lightcoral;
        padding: 20px;
        border-radius: 5px;
        text-align: center;
        width: 150px;
        height: 150px;
    }
  </style>
</head>
<body>
  <div class="flex-container">
    <div class="flex-item">Item 1</div>
    <div class="flex-item">Item 2</div>
    <div class="flex-item">Item 3</div>
  </div>
</body>
</html>
```

Explanation:

- .flex-container is the flex container with display: flex;, aligning items horizontally (justify-content: space-between) with space between the items, and centering them vertically (align-items: center).

- Each .flex-item is styled with some padding, a background color, and set width/height.

When resizing the browser window, the items will automatically distribute themselves evenly across the available space.

CSS Grid: A Two-Dimensional Layout Model

CSS Grid Layout is a powerful layout system for creating complex, two-dimensional web layouts. It allows you to design both rows and columns simultaneously, giving you more control over both axes of the layout. While Flexbox is great for one-dimensional layouts, Grid is perfect for complex layouts that require precise control over both the vertical and horizontal axes.

Key Concepts in CSS Grid

1. **Grid Container**: The parent element that becomes a grid. You define it with display: grid;.
2. **Grid Items**: The child elements inside the grid container. These elements are placed into specific grid cells defined by the grid.

Properties of the Grid Container

- display: grid;: Turns the container into a grid.

- grid-template-columns and grid-template-rows: These properties define the number of columns and rows, respectively. You can specify them in absolute units like px or em, or use flexible units like fr (fractional units).

- grid-gap: Sets the space between rows and columns in the grid.

- grid-template-areas: Allows you to assign names to areas of the grid for a more readable layout.

- align-items: Aligns the grid items along the block (vertical) axis.

- justify-items: Aligns the grid items along the inline (horizontal) axis.

- grid-auto-rows and grid-auto-columns: Controls the size of rows and columns that are created automatically when there are more items than the defined grid.

Example: Basic CSS Grid Layout

Let's create a responsive layout using CSS Grid with both rows and columns.

html

```
<!DOCTYPE html>
<html lang="en">
```

```html
<head>
    <meta charset="UTF-8">
    <meta name="viewport" content="width=device-width, initial-scale=1.0">
    <title>CSS Grid Layout Example</title>
    <style>
        .grid-container {
            display: grid;
            grid-template-columns: repeat(3, 1fr);
            grid-gap: 20px;
            padding: 20px;
            background-color: #f4f4f4;
        }
        .grid-item {
            background-color: lightseagreen;
            padding: 20px;
            text-align: center;
            color: white;
            font-size: 1.2em;
        }
    </style>
</head>
<body>
    <div class="grid-container">
        <div class="grid-item">Item 1</div>
        <div class="grid-item">Item 2</div>
        <div class="grid-item">Item 3</div>
        <div class="grid-item">Item 4</div>
        <div class="grid-item">Item 5</div>
        <div class="grid-item">Item 6</div>
    </div>
```

```
</body>
</html>
```

Explanation:

- The .grid-container is set up with display: grid;, defining 3 equal columns with grid-template-columns: repeat(3, 1fr); (each column takes up 1 fraction of the available space).

- grid-gap: 20px; adds spacing between the grid items.

As the browser window shrinks, the grid items will automatically adjust their size and alignment, thanks to the flexible nature of CSS Grid.

Combining Flexbox and Grid: Real-World Example

In many real-world scenarios, you may want to combine both Flexbox and Grid for different parts of your layout. For example, you could use **CSS Grid** for the main structure of the page (like the header, sidebar, and content area), and use **Flexbox** inside specific sections, like a navigation menu or a row of products.

Here's a simple example of combining both:

html

```
<!DOCTYPE html>
<html lang="en">
<head>
```

```html
<meta charset="UTF-8">
<meta name="viewport" content="width=device-width, initial-scale=1.0">
<title>Responsive Layout with Grid and Flexbox</title>
<style>
  /* Grid container */
  .container {
    display: grid;
    grid-template-columns: 1fr 3fr;
    grid-gap: 20px;
    padding: 20px;
    background-color: #f9f9f9;
  }

  /* Flexbox inside a grid item */
  .sidebar {
    display: flex;
    flex-direction: column;
    gap: 10px;
  }

  .content {
    display: flex;
    flex-wrap: wrap;
    gap: 20px;
  }

  .item {
    background-color: lightcoral;
    padding: 20px;
    width: 200px;
```

```
            text-align: center;
            border-radius: 5px;
        }
    </style>
</head>
<body>
    <div class="container">
        <div class="sidebar">
            <div>Link 1</div>
            <div>Link 2</div>
            <div>Link 3</div>
        </div>
        <div class="content">
            <div class="item">Item 1</div>
            <div class="item">Item 2</div>
            <div class="item">Item 3</div>
        </div>
    </div>
</body>
</html>
```

Explanation:

- The main layout uses grid-template-columns: 1fr 3fr; to create a two-column structure, with the sidebar taking up one fraction of space and the content area taking up three.

- Inside the .sidebar, Flexbox is used to stack the links vertically.

- Inside the .content, Flexbox is used to display items in a flexible grid that wraps if necessary.

This combination allows for greater flexibility and responsiveness in more complex layouts.

In this chapter, we covered two essential layout techniques: **Flexbox** and **CSS Grid**. Flexbox is ideal for simpler, one-dimensional layouts, while CSS Grid is perfect for complex, two-dimensional layouts. Understanding when and how to use these two tools will help you create modern, responsive websites with ease.

In the next chapter, we'll dive deeper into **advanced CSS techniques** such as animations, transitions, and custom properties, which will allow you to add interactivity and dynamic effects to your layouts.

CHAPTER 7: ADVANCED CSS STYLING

CSS is a powerful tool that allows developers to craft visually compelling and highly interactive web pages. In this chapter, we'll explore more advanced aspects of CSS, including **pseudo-classes, pseudo-elements, CSS transitions, animations,** and **custom properties (CSS variables)**. These techniques enable you to add interactive elements, dynamic effects, and reusable styles that can significantly improve both the aesthetics and user experience of your website.

1. Pseudo-Classes and Pseudo-Elements

CSS **pseudo-classes** and **pseudo-elements** allow you to apply styles to elements in ways that are not possible with simple selectors. They can be used to style an element based on its state (e.g., when it's hovered over or focused on) or to target specific parts of an element, like the first letter or line of text.

Pseudo-Classes

- :hover: Applies styles when an element is hovered over by the cursor. Typically used for interactive elements like links or buttons.
- :focus: Applies styles when an element is focused (such as when a user clicks on an input field or navigates to it using the keyboard).
- :nth-child(n): Selects elements based on their position in a parent container. You can target specific child elements, even based on mathematical formulas (e.g., :nth-child(odd) or :nth-child(3)).
- :first-child, :last-child: Selects the first or last child of a parent element.
- :active: Applies styles when an element is in an active state (such as when a button is clicked).

Pseudo-Elements

- ::before: Inserts content before an element's actual content. It's often used for adding decorative icons, quotation marks, or other content.
- ::after: Inserts content after an element's actual content, often used for creating effects like clearing floats.
- ::first-letter: Targets the first letter of a block of text, allowing you to apply different styles to the first character (like a drop cap).
- ::first-line: Targets the first line of text inside a block-level element.

Example: Using Pseudo-Classes and Pseudo-Elements

html

```
<!DOCTYPE html>
<html lang="en">
<head>
  <meta charset="UTF-8">
  <meta name="viewport" content="width=device-width, initial-scale=1.0">
  <title>Pseudo-Classes and Pseudo-Elements</title>
  <style>
    /* Basic Styling */
    .button {
      background-color: #007BFF;
      color: white;
      padding: 10px 20px;
```

```css
  border: none;
  cursor: pointer;
  border-radius: 5px;
}

/* Hover State */
.button:hover {
  background-color: #0056b3;
}

/* Focus State */
.input:focus {
  border: 2px solid #0056b3;
  outline: none;
}

/* Using nth-child */
ul li:nth-child(odd) {
  background-color: #f2f2f2;
}

/* Before Pseudo-element */
.quote::before {
  content: "";
  font-size: 2em;
  color: #007BFF;
}

/* After Pseudo-element */
.quote::after {
```

```
        content: "";
        font-size: 2em;
        color: #007BFF;
      }
    </style>
  </head>
  <body>
    <button class="button">Hover Over Me</button>
    <input class="input" type="text" placeholder="Focus Me">
    <ul>
      <li>Item 1</li>
      <li>Item 2</li>
      <li>Item 3</li>
      <li>Item 4</li>
    </ul>
    <blockquote class="quote">CSS is a powerful tool.</blockquote>
  </body>
</html>
```

In this example:

- We used :hover to change the button color on hover.
- :focus changes the border color when the input field is focused.
- The ::before and ::after pseudo-elements are used to add quotation marks around the text.

2. CSS Transitions and Animations

Transitions and animations are key to creating engaging, interactive websites. They allow you to animate the changes between styles, giving the page a sense of interactivity and smoothness.

CSS Transitions

CSS **transitions** provide a way to smoothly change from one style to another when a property value changes. You define the initial state and the end state, and CSS automatically interpolates the difference between them.

Key properties of CSS transitions:

- transition-property: Specifies the CSS property to be transitioned.
- transition-duration: Defines how long the transition takes to complete.
- transition-timing-function: Defines the speed curve of the transition. Common values are linear, ease, ease-in, ease-out, and ease-in-out.
- transition-delay: Defines the delay before the transition starts.

Example: Button Hover with Transition

html

```
<!DOCTYPE html>
<html lang="en">
<head>
```

```html
<meta charset="UTF-8">
<meta name="viewport" content="width=device-width, initial-scale=1.0">
<title>Button Transition Example</title>
<style>
    .button {
        background-color: #28a745;
        color: white;
        padding: 10px 20px;
        border: none;
        border-radius: 5px;
        cursor: pointer;
        transition: background-color 0.3s ease, transform 0.2s ease;
    }

    .button:hover {
        background-color: #218838;
        transform: scale(1.1);
    }
</style>
</head>
<body>
    <button class="button">Hover Over Me</button>
</body>
</html>
```

In this example:

- The button smoothly changes its background color and scales up slightly when hovered over, thanks to the transition property.

- transition: background-color 0.3s ease, transform 0.2s ease; specifies both properties to animate and their respective durations and timing functions.

CSS Animations

While transitions are great for state changes, **animations** allow you to create more complex and continuous movements. CSS animations use @keyframes to define the sequence of style changes.

Key properties of CSS animations:

- @keyframes: Defines the animation's steps.
- animation-name: Specifies the name of the animation.
- animation-duration: Defines how long the animation runs.
- animation-timing-function: Similar to transitions, it defines the easing of the animation.
- animation-delay: Adds a delay before the animation starts.
- animation-iteration-count: Specifies how many times the animation should repeat (e.g., infinite for continuous animation).

Example: Simple Fade-In Animation

html

```
<!DOCTYPE html>
<html lang="en">
<head>
  <meta charset="UTF-8">
```

```html
<meta name="viewport" content="width=device-width, initial-scale=1.0">
<title>CSS Fade-In Animation</title>
<style>
    /* Define the keyframe for fade-in */
    @keyframes fadeIn {
        0% {
            opacity: 0;
        }
        100% {
            opacity: 1;
        }
    }

    .box {
        width: 200px;
        height: 200px;
        background-color: #007BFF;
        animation: fadeIn 2s ease-in-out;
    }
</style>
</head>
<body>
    <div class="box"></div>
</body>
</html>
```

In this example:

- The @keyframes fadeIn defines the animation sequence, starting from opacity: 0 (invisible) and ending at opacity: 1 (fully visible).

- The animation: fadeIn 2s ease-in-out; applies the animation to the .box element.

---

3. Custom Properties (CSS Variables)

CSS variables, also known as **custom properties,** allow you to define reusable values throughout your CSS, making your stylesheets cleaner and more maintainable. They enable dynamic changes to properties at runtime and can be overridden in specific contexts.

Defining and Using Custom Properties

- You define a variable using --variable-name syntax.
- You access the variable using var(--variable-name).

Example: Using CSS Variables for Theming

html

```
<!DOCTYPE html>
<html lang="en">
<head>
  <meta charset="UTF-8">
  <meta name="viewport" content="width=device-width, initial-scale=1.0">
  <title>CSS Variables Example</title>
  <style>
    /* Define variables at the root level */
    :root {
```

```css
    --primary-color: #28a745;
    --secondary-color: #dc3545;
    --font-family: Arial, sans-serif;
  }

  body {
    font-family: var(--font-family);
  }

  .button {
    background-color: var(--primary-color);
    color: white;
    padding: 10px 20px;
    border: none;
    border-radius: 5px;
  }

  .button-danger {
    background-color: var(--secondary-color);
  }
  </style>
</head>
<body>
  <button class="button">Primary Button</button>
  <button class="button button-danger">Danger Button</button>
</body>
</html>
```

In this example:

- Custom properties --primary-color, --secondary-color, and --font-family are defined at the root level and used throughout the stylesheet.

- The .button class uses the --primary-color for the background, while .button-danger uses --secondary-color.

In this chapter, we explored advanced CSS techniques such as **pseudo-classes** and **pseudo-elements**, which allow for more targeted and dynamic styling, as well as **CSS transitions** and **animations**, which enable you to create smooth, interactive changes. We also covered **CSS variables** (custom properties), a powerful tool for maintaining clean and flexible stylesheets. These techniques will give you greater control over the look and feel of your website, allowing you to create more engaging, responsive, and interactive user experiences.

In the next chapter, we will dive into **JavaScript**, the final key component of front-end development, and how it integrates with HTML and CSS to bring dynamic functionality to web pages.

CHAPTER 8: INTRODUCTION TO JAVASCRIPT – PROGRAMMING THE WEB

JavaScript is the programming language that powers interactivity on the web. While HTML provides structure and CSS provides style, JavaScript is what makes a webpage dynamic and interactive. In this chapter, we will explore the fundamentals of JavaScript, including its basic syntax, data types, operators, and control flow. These core concepts will provide the foundation for building more complex and interactive features as you advance in your web development journey.

1. What is JavaScript?

JavaScript is a high-level, interpreted programming language primarily used to create interactive effects within web browsers. While HTML structures content and CSS defines the look and feel, JavaScript adds behavior, allowing you to respond to user actions, manipulate the DOM (Document Object Model), and even make requests to servers without reloading the page (using AJAX).

JavaScript runs in the browser, which makes it a client-side language, although it can also run on the server with environments like Node.js. It can be used to create things like:

- Form validation
- Image sliders
- Dynamic content updates
- Interactive maps
- Animations
- Games and web apps

In short, JavaScript allows you to bring life and interactivity to static HTML and CSS pages.

2. Basic Syntax and Data Types

Before diving into more complex topics, let's first look at the building blocks of JavaScript: **syntax** and **data types**.

Basic Syntax

- **Statements:** JavaScript code is made up of statements, which are executed in order. Each statement ends with a semicolon (;), although it's not strictly required.
- **Comments:** You can write comments in JavaScript using // for single-line comments or /* */ for multi-line comments.

javascript

```
// This is a single-line comment
/* This is a
multi-line comment */
```

Variables

Variables store data values. In JavaScript, you can declare variables using var, let, or const.

- var: Historically used, but now generally avoided due to issues with scoping.
- let: The modern way to declare variables with block scope (can be re-assigned).
- const: Declares a constant variable that cannot be re-assigned.

javascript

```
let name = "John";  // A variable that can be changed
const age = 30;     // A constant that can't be reassigned
```

Data Types

JavaScript supports several fundamental data types:

- **String:** Text values, wrapped in single (') or double (") quotes.

- **Number:** Numeric values, either integers or floating-point numbers.

- **Boolean:** True or false values.

- **Array:** An ordered collection of values, which can be of any data type.

- **Object:** A collection of key-value pairs, often used for representing more complex data.

javascript

```
let name = "Alice";     // String
let age = 25;           // Number
let isStudent = true;   // Boolean
let colors = ["red", "green", "blue"]; // Array
let person = {name: "John", age: 30};  // Object
```

---

3. Operators and Control Flow

Operators

Operators in JavaScript are used to perform operations on variables and values. There are several types of operators:

- **Arithmetic Operators:** Used for mathematical calculations.
    - + (Addition)
    - - (Subtraction)
    - * (Multiplication)
    - / (Division)
    - % (Modulus)
    - ++ (Increment)
    - -- (Decrement)

javascript

```
let x = 5;
let y = 3;
let sum = x + y;  // 8
let product = x * y;  // 15
```

- **Comparison Operators:** Used to compare values and return a Boolean (true or false).
    - == (Equal to)
    - != (Not equal to)
    - > (Greater than)
    - < (Less than)
    - >= (Greater than or equal to)

    o   <= (Less than or equal to)

javascript

```
let a = 10;
let b = 5;
let result = a > b;  // true
```

- **Logical Operators:** Used to combine multiple conditions.
  - && (AND)
  - || (OR)
  - ! (NOT)

javascript

```
let isAdult = true;
let isEmployed = false;
let canVote = isAdult && isEmployed; // false
```

Control Flow

Control flow statements allow you to control the execution of code based on conditions or repetition. These include:

- **Conditional Statements (if, else, switch):**
  - if: Executes a block of code if a condition is true.
  - else: Executes a block of code if the condition in the if statement is false.
  - switch: Evaluates an expression and matches the value against multiple cases.

javascript

```javascript
let age = 20;

if (age >= 18) {
  console.log("You are an adult.");
} else {
  console.log("You are a minor.");
}

let day = 3;
switch(day) {
  case 1:
    console.log("Monday");
    break;
  case 2:
    console.log("Tuesday");
    break;
  default:
    console.log("Weekend");
}
```

- **Loops (for, while):**
  - for: Loops through a block of code a certain number of times.
  - while: Loops through a block of code as long as the condition is true.

javascript

```
// for loop: printing numbers from 1 to 5
for (let i = 1; i <= 5; i++) {
    console.log(i);
}
```

```
// while loop: printing numbers from 5 to 1
let i = 5;
while (i >= 1) {
    console.log(i);
    i--;
}
```

4. Real-World Example: Writing a Basic JavaScript Function to Calculate User Input

Let's now create a simple JavaScript function that takes user input and calculates a result based on it. For this example, we'll write a function that calculates the total price of items in a shopping cart after applying a discount.

html

```
<!DOCTYPE html>
<html lang="en">
<head>
    <meta charset="UTF-8">
    <meta name="viewport" content="width=device-width, initial-scale=1.0">
    <title>Shopping Cart Calculator</title>
</head>
<body>
```

```
<h1>Shopping Cart Total</h1>
<label for="price">Item Price ($): </label>
<input type="number" id="price" placeholder="Enter price">

<label for="quantity">Quantity: </label>
<input type="number" id="quantity" placeholder="Enter quantity">

<label for="discount">Discount (%)</label>
<input type="number" id="discount" placeholder="Enter discount">

<button onclick="calculateTotal()">Calculate Total</button>

<p id="total">Total: $0</p>

<script>
    function calculateTotal() {
        // Get values from the inputs
        let price = parseFloat(document.getElementById("price").value);
        let quantity = parseInt(document.getElementById("quantity").value);
        let discount = parseFloat(document.getElementById("discount").value);

        // Check if the values are valid
        if (isNaN(price) || isNaN(quantity) || isNaN(discount)) {
            alert("Please enter valid numbers.");
            return;
        }

        // Calculate the total
        let totalPrice = price * quantity;
        let discountAmount = (totalPrice * discount) / 100;
```

```
        let finalPrice = totalPrice - discountAmount;

        // Display the result
        document.getElementById("total").textContent    =    "Total:    $"    +
finalPrice.toFixed(2);
    }
  </script>
</body>
</html>
```

Explanation:

- The user enters the **price**, **quantity**, and **discount** in the input fields.
- The calculateTotal() function:
    1. Retrieves the values from the input fields.
    2. Calculates the total price by multiplying the price and quantity.
    3. Computes the discount amount and subtracts it from the total.
    4. Displays the final price.

In this chapter, we introduced **JavaScript** as the language that brings interactivity and dynamic behavior to websites. We covered basic **syntax** and **data types**, and explored **operators** and **control**

flow structures like conditionals and loops. Finally, we wrote a real-world example that used JavaScript to handle user input and perform calculations.

With these foundational concepts, you are now ready to start adding dynamic features to your websites. In the next chapter, we'll dive deeper into JavaScript functions, how to handle events, and how to manipulate the DOM (Document Object Model) to dynamically change page content.

CHAPTER 9: FUNCTIONS AND EVENTS IN JAVASCRIPT

In this chapter, we will dive into two fundamental concepts of JavaScript: **functions** and **events**. Functions allow you to organize your code into reusable blocks, making it easier to manage and maintain. Events, on the other hand, bring interactivity to your website by responding to user actions such as clicks, mouse movements, or keyboard input. By mastering these concepts, you'll be able to write more efficient code and create interactive, user-friendly websites.

---

1. Defining Functions: How to Create and Use Functions to Organize Your Code

A **function** in JavaScript is a block of code designed to perform a particular task. Functions are useful because they allow you to avoid repeating the same code multiple times, making your code cleaner, more efficient, and easier to maintain. Functions can take inputs, known as parameters, and return outputs, which can be used in other parts of your code.

Syntax of a Function

The basic syntax of a function looks like this:

javascript

```javascript
function functionName(parameters) {
    // Code to execute
    return result;  // Optional: Return a value
}
```

- functionName: The name of the function (choose descriptive names that indicate the function's purpose).
- parameters: Optional inputs that the function can accept (can be none, one, or more).

- return: Optional: The value that the function sends back to the calling code. If omitted, the function returns undefined.

Example: Simple Function

Let's start by defining a function that adds two numbers:

javascript

```
function addNumbers(a, b) {
    return a + b;
}

// Call the function with arguments
let sum = addNumbers(5, 3);
console.log(sum);  // Output: 8
```

In this example:

- addNumbers is the function that takes two parameters, a and b.
- The function returns the sum of a and b.
- The function is called with the arguments 5 and 3, and the result is stored in the sum variable.

Function Expressions

In addition to function declarations, JavaScript also allows you to create functions using function expressions:

javascript

```
const multiply = function(a, b) {
```

```
    return a * b;
};
```

```
let result = multiply(4, 6);
console.log(result);  // Output: 24
```

This is an anonymous function assigned to the multiply variable. The function behaves just like the previous example but is created as part of an expression.

Arrow Functions (ES6+)

With ES6 (ECMAScript 2015), JavaScript introduced arrow functions, which provide a more concise syntax for writing functions:

javascript

```
const subtract = (a, b) => a - b;
```

```
let difference = subtract(10, 5);
console.log(difference);  // Output: 5
```

Arrow functions are particularly useful for small functions and help reduce boilerplate code.

---

2. Event Handling: Adding Interactivity with JavaScript Events

Events are actions that happen in the browser, such as user interactions (clicking, typing, or moving the mouse) or other occurrences like page loading. JavaScript allows you to attach event listeners to elements on the page, so when the event occurs, JavaScript responds by executing a function.

Common JavaScript Events

Here are some common JavaScript events that are used to trigger functions:

- **click**: Triggered when an element is clicked.
- **mouseover**: Triggered when the mouse pointer hovers over an element.
- **keydown**: Triggered when a key is pressed.
- **submit**: Triggered when a form is submitted.

Attaching Event Listeners

To make your page interactive, you need to attach event listeners to specific elements. This can be done using JavaScript's addEventListener() method, which allows you to specify which event should trigger the function.

javascript

```
document.getElementById("myButton").addEventListener("click", function() {
   alert("Button was clicked!");
});
```

In this example:

- getElementById("myButton"): Selects the HTML element with the id of "myButton".

- addEventListener("click", function() {...}): Adds an event listener for the click event, which triggers the anonymous function when the button is clicked.

Event Handler as a Function

Instead of using an anonymous function, you can reference a predefined function:

javascript

```
function showMessage() {
    alert("Hello, world!");
}
```

```
document.getElementById("myButton").addEventListener("click",
showMessage);
```

This example defines a function (showMessage) and passes it to the addEventListener method. When the button is clicked, the showMessage function is executed.

Mouse Events and More

You can also handle mouse events such as mouseover, mouseout, and mousemove to respond to mouse interactions:

javascript

```
document.getElementById("myElement").addEventListener("mouseover",
function() {
    console.log("Mouse is over the element!");
```

});

---

3. Real-World Example: Adding a Button that Changes the Background Color When Clicked

Now, let's put everything together by creating an interactive web page where clicking a button changes the background color. We will use both **functions** and **event handling** to achieve this.

HTML Code:

html

```
<!DOCTYPE html>
<html lang="en">
<head>
  <meta charset="UTF-8">
  <meta name="viewport" content="width=device-width, initial-scale=1.0">
  <title>Change Background Color</title>
  <style>
    body {
      font-family: Arial, sans-serif;
      text-align: center;
      padding: 50px;
    }
    #colorButton {
      padding: 10px 20px;
      font-size: 16px;
      cursor: pointer;
      background-color: #4CAF50;
      color: white;
```

```
      border: none;
      border-radius: 5px;
   }
  </style>
</head>
<body>

  <h1>Click the Button to Change Background Color</h1>
  <button id="colorButton">Change Color</button>

  <script>
    // Function to change the background color
    function changeBackgroundColor() {
      // Generate a random color
      const            randomColor         =            "#"           +
Math.floor(Math.random()*16777215).toString(16);
        // Apply the random color to the body's background
        document.body.style.backgroundColor = randomColor;
      }

    // Attach an event listener to the button
    document.getElementById("colorButton").addEventListener("click",
changeBackgroundColor);
  </script>

</body>
</html>
```

Explanation:

1. **HTML**:

o We create a simple webpage with a button element
(<button id="colorButton">).

2. **CSS**:

   o We add some basic styling to center the content and
   style the button.

3. **JavaScript**:

   o The changeBackgroundColor function generates a
   random color using Math.random() and applies it to
   the page's background by setting the
   style.backgroundColor property.

   o We attach an event listener to the #colorButton
   element using addEventListener, so that every time the
   button is clicked, the changeBackgroundColor function
   is executed.

In this chapter, we introduced the concept of **functions** and how
they help organize code, making it reusable and easier to maintain.
We also explored **event handling**, which allows your web pages to
respond to user interactions like clicks, mouse movements, and
keyboard input. By combining these two concepts, we created a
simple interactive feature that changes the background color of a
page when a button is clicked.

As you continue learning, you'll be able to build more complex interactive features by combining multiple event listeners and JavaScript functions. In the next chapter, we will delve deeper into manipulating the **DOM** (Document Object Model), which is essential for dynamically changing HTML content based on user actions or other events.

CHAPTER 10: WORKING WITH THE DOM (DOCUMENT OBJECT MODEL)

In this chapter, we will explore one of the most essential concepts in front-end web development: the **Document Object Model (DOM)**. The DOM allows JavaScript to interact with and manipulate HTML and CSS, turning static web pages into dynamic, interactive experiences. By understanding how the DOM works, you can create more engaging and responsive web pages.

1. Understanding the DOM: How JavaScript Interacts with HTML and CSS via the DOM

The **DOM** is an interface that represents the structure of an HTML document as a tree of objects. Every element, attribute, and piece of text within a web page is a node in this tree. JavaScript uses the DOM to interact with HTML and CSS, allowing you to dynamically update the content, structure, and styling of a webpage.

In simple terms, the DOM acts as a bridge between the static content of your web page (HTML) and the dynamic behavior you want to create (JavaScript).

Example:

- HTML: <h1>Hello, world!</h1>
- In the DOM: The <h1> tag is represented as an object that JavaScript can interact with.

The DOM Tree

- The DOM is a hierarchical structure with a root node (<html>), child nodes representing elements like <body>, <div>, and <p>, and further descendant nodes representing the actual content (text nodes, attributes, etc.).

- This structure allows JavaScript to navigate, find, and manipulate elements.

For instance, JavaScript can access the body element of a webpage using document.body, and then it can drill down further to find specific tags like <p> or <img>.

---

2.   *Selecting   Elements: Using   getElementById, getElementsByClassName, and querySelector*

To manipulate elements using JavaScript, the first step is selecting them from the DOM. There are several methods available for selecting elements based on different criteria.

getElementById

This method is used to select an element by its unique ID.

javascript

```
const heading = document.getElementById('myHeading');
heading.style.color = 'blue';   // Changes the color of the element with id 'myHeading'
```

- **Use case**: You should use this method when you know the element's ID, which should be unique within the page.

getElementsByClassName

This method selects all elements with a specific class name and returns them as a live HTMLCollection.

javascript

```
const buttons = document.getElementsByClassName('btn');
buttons[0].style.backgroundColor = 'green';  // Changes the background color of
the first element with class 'btn'
```

- **Use case**: Useful when you need to work with a group of elements that share the same class.

querySelector

This method selects the first element that matches a given CSS selector, which allows more flexibility (e.g., selecting by class, ID, or attribute).

javascript

```
const firstButton = document.querySelector('.btn');
firstButton.style.fontSize = '20px';  // Changes the font size of the first element
with class 'btn'
```

- **Use case**: It's versatile and more modern, as it can target almost any valid CSS selector (class, ID, tag, etc.).

querySelectorAll

If you need to select all elements that match a specific CSS selector, querySelectorAll returns a **NodeList** of all matching elements.

javascript

```
const allButtons = document.querySelectorAll('.btn');
allButtons.forEach(button => {
    button.style.color = 'red';  // Changes the text color of all elements with class 'btn'
});
```

---

3. Manipulating Elements: Changing Text, Styles, and Content Dynamically

Once you've selected an element, JavaScript allows you to manipulate it in various ways. You can change its content, styles, attributes, and more.

Changing Text Content

You can change the text of an element using the .textContent property:

javascript

```
const paragraph = document.getElementById('para');
paragraph.textContent = 'This is a new text content!';
```

- **textContent**: Sets or retrieves the plain text inside an element.

Changing HTML Content

You can also modify an element's HTML content (including tags) using .innerHTML:

javascript

```
const div = document.getElementById('myDiv');
div.innerHTML = '<p>This is <strong>new</strong> content!</p>';
```

- **innerHTML**: Allows you to get or set the HTML markup inside an element.

Modifying Styles

To modify an element's styles, use the .style property, which allows you to access and change inline styles:

javascript

```
const box = document.getElementById('myBox');
box.style.backgroundColor = 'yellow';   // Changes the background color to yellow
box.style.width = '200px';          // Changes the width to 200px
```

- **style**: Directly modifies the element's inline styles. This can only change styles defined in the style attribute and doesn't affect external or internal stylesheets.

Adding and Removing Classes

A more flexible way to change an element's style is by adding or removing CSS classes:

javascript

```
const button = document.querySelector('#submitButton');
button.classList.add('active');  // Adds the 'active' class
button.classList.remove('disabled');  // Removes the 'disabled' class
```

- **classList**: Provides methods like add(), remove(), and toggle() to modify the classes of an element.

---

4. Real-World Example: Creating a To-Do List Where Items Are Added and Removed Dynamically

Let's use everything we've learned so far to build a simple **to-do list** application. The list will allow users to add and remove tasks dynamically using JavaScript, manipulating the DOM based on user input.

HTML Code:

html

```
<!DOCTYPE html>
<html lang="en">
<head>
    <meta charset="UTF-8">
    <meta name="viewport" content="width=device-width, initial-scale=1.0">
    <title>To-Do List</title>
```

```
<style>
  body {
    font-family: Arial, sans-serif;
    max-width: 500px;
    margin: auto;
    padding: 20px;
    background-color: #f4f4f4;
  }
  #todoInput {
    padding: 10px;
    width: 80%;
    margin-bottom: 10px;
  }
  #addButton {
    padding: 10px 20px;
    background-color: #4CAF50;
    color: white;
    border: none;
    cursor: pointer;
  }
  .todoItem {
    background-color: #fff;
    padding: 10px;
    margin-bottom: 10px;
    border: 1px solid #ddd;
    display: flex;
    justify-content: space-between;
  }
  .removeBtn {
    color: red;
```

```
      cursor: pointer;
    }
  </style>
</head>
<body>

  <h2>To-Do List</h2>
  <input type="text" id="todoInput" placeholder="Add a new task">
  <button id="addButton">Add Task</button>

  <ul id="todoList"></ul>

  <script>
    // Function to add a new task
    function addTask() {
      const todoInput = document.getElementById('todoInput');
      const taskText = todoInput.value.trim();

      if (taskText === "") {
        alert("Please enter a task!");
        return;
      }

      const todoList = document.getElementById('todoList');

      // Create new list item
      const li = document.createElement('li');
      li.classList.add('todoItem');

      // Add task text
```

```
    li.textContent = taskText;

    // Create remove button
    const removeBtn = document.createElement('span');
    removeBtn.textContent = 'Remove';
    removeBtn.classList.add('removeBtn');
    removeBtn.addEventListener('click', function() {
        li.remove();
    });

    // Append remove button to the list item
    li.appendChild(removeBtn);

    // Append the new item to the list
    todoList.appendChild(li);

    // Clear the input field
    todoInput.value = "";
}

// Event listener for the Add Task button
document.getElementById('addButton').addEventListener('click', addTask);

// Allow pressing Enter to add a task
document.getElementById('todoInput').addEventListener('keypress',
function(e) {
    if (e.key === 'Enter') {
        addTask();
    }
});
```

```
</script>

</body>
</html>
```

Explanation:

- **HTML**: We define an input field (#todoInput) for entering new tasks, a button (#addButton) to add tasks, and an empty <ul> (#todoList) where tasks will be listed.
- **CSS**: Basic styles for the page, including input field and button styles, as well as styles for the tasks and the remove button.
- **JavaScript**:
  - The addTask function reads the input value, creates a new <li> element with the task text, and appends a "Remove" button to each new task.
  - When the "Remove" button is clicked, the corresponding task item is removed from the list.
  - We also listen for the Enter key, allowing the user to add a task by pressing it.

In this chapter, we've covered the basics of interacting with the DOM using JavaScript. We learned how to select elements using methods like getElementById, querySelector, and querySelectorAll, and we explored how to manipulate elements by changing their content, styles, and classes. Finally, we built a practical **to-do list** app, applying our knowledge of the DOM to create dynamic web pages that respond to user input.

Mastering the DOM is a critical skill for any front-end developer, as it opens the door to creating highly interactive and dynamic websites. In the next chapter, we'll dive deeper into **advanced DOM manipulation** techniques, such as working with forms and dynamically creating and removing elements.

CHAPTER 11: FORMS AND VALIDATION IN JAVASCRIPT

Forms are an essential part of web applications. They allow users to submit data, which can be processed or stored on a server. As a front-end developer, one of your core responsibilities is ensuring that forms are functional and secure. In this chapter, we'll cover the key concepts and techniques you need to handle forms and validate user input effectively using **HTML** and **JavaScript**.

---

1. Form Elements in JavaScript: Working with *<form>*, *<input>*, *<textarea>*, and Other Elements

HTML forms consist of various form elements, including text fields, checkboxes, radio buttons, buttons, and more. These elements allow users to input data that can be submitted to a server or processed by JavaScript.

Form Elements:

1. **<form>**: The <form> element wraps all the form inputs and controls. It's the container for all form elements and defines the form's submission behavior.

    o   Example: <form id="contactForm"> ... </form>

2. **<input>**: This is the most common form element, used for text fields, checkboxes, radio buttons, and more.

   o Example: <input type="text" id="name" name="name">

3. **<textarea>**: Used for multi-line text input, such as messages or comments.

   o Example: <textarea id="message" name="message"></textarea>

4. **<select> and <option>**: These elements are used to create dropdown lists for selecting options.

   o Example:

   html

   ```
   <select id="country" name="country">
     <option value="us">USA</option>
     <option value="uk">UK</option>
   </select>
   ```

5. **<button>**: Used to trigger form submissions or other actions in JavaScript.

   o Example: <button type="submit">Submit</button>

Accessing Form Elements in JavaScript:

Once the form is created, JavaScript can be used to interact with its elements. You can select form elements using methods like getElementById or querySelector, and then read or modify their values.

javascript

```
const nameInput = document.getElementById('name');
console.log(nameInput.value);  // Get the value of the input field
```

You can also attach event listeners to form elements to listen for actions like submit, input, or change.

---

2. Form Validation: Validating User Input

Before submitting a form, it's important to validate the user input to ensure that it meets the required criteria (e.g., ensuring a field is filled out, checking email format, or enforcing password strength).

Why Validation Is Important:

- **Client-Side Validation**: Ensures that users provide valid input before the data is submitted to the server, reducing errors and unnecessary server load.
- **Security**: Prevents malicious input, such as SQL injection or cross-site scripting (XSS) attacks, by ensuring only sanitized data is sent.

Basic Validation Techniques:

1. **Checking Required Fields**:
   o   Ensure a field is not left empty.

   javascript

```javascript
const nameInput = document.getElementById('name');
if (nameInput.value === "") {
  alert("Name is required!");
  return false;  // Prevent form submission
}
```

2. **Email Validation**:

- o You can use regular expressions (regex) to validate an email address format.

javascript

```javascript
const emailInput = document.getElementById('email');
const emailPattern = /^[a-zA-Z0-9._-]+@[a-zA-Z0-9.-]+\.[a-zA-Z]{2,6}$/;
if (!emailPattern.test(emailInput.value)) {
  alert("Please enter a valid email address.");
  return false;
}
```

3. **Password Strength**:

- o Passwords often require a minimum length or complexity (e.g., including uppercase letters, numbers, or special characters).

javascript

```javascript
const passwordInput = document.getElementById('password');
const password = passwordInput.value;
```

```
if (password.length  <  8  ||  !/[A-Z]/.test(password)  ||  !/[0-
9]/.test(password)) {
    alert("Password must be at least 8 characters long and contain a
number and an uppercase letter.");
    return false;
}
```

4. **Checking for Matching Passwords**:

o Ensure that the "confirm password" field matches the first password input.

javascript

```
const                   confirmPasswordInput                   =
document.getElementById('confirmPassword');
if (password !== confirmPasswordInput.value) {
    alert("Passwords do not match.");
    return false;
}
```

Built-in HTML5 Validation:

In addition to custom JavaScript validation, HTML5 provides built-in form validation attributes, such as:

- **required**: Ensures a field is not empty.

- **pattern**: Specifies a regular expression the input must match.

- **minlength and maxlength**: Defines the minimum and maximum allowed length for a text field.

html

```
<form id="signupForm">
    <input type="email" id="email" name="email" required placeholder="Email">
    <input type="password" id="password" name="password" minlength="8" required placeholder="Password">
    <input type="password" id="confirmPassword" name="confirmPassword" required placeholder="Confirm Password">
    <button type="submit">Sign Up</button>
</form>
```

With the required and minlength attributes, the browser will automatically alert the user if these fields are not filled in correctly.

---

3. Real-World Example: Building a Contact Form with Validation

Let's put everything together by building a simple **contact form** that validates the user's input before submission. The form will include fields for a name, email, message, and a submit button. We'll use JavaScript to ensure the user enters a valid email address and that the message field is not empty.

HTML Code:

html

```
<!DOCTYPE html>
<html lang="en">
```

```
<head>
   <meta charset="UTF-8">
   <meta name="viewport" content="width=device-width, initial-scale=1.0">
   <title>Contact Form</title>
   <style>
      body { font-family: Arial, sans-serif; margin: 20px; }
      .form-field { margin-bottom: 15px; }
      label { display: block; margin-bottom: 5px; }
      input, textarea { width: 100%; padding: 8px; font-size: 16px; }
      button { padding: 10px 20px; background-color: #4CAF50; color: white;
border: none; cursor: pointer; }
   </style>
</head>
<body>

<h2>Contact Us</h2>
<form id="contactForm">
   <div class="form-field">
      <label for="name">Your Name</label>
      <input type="text" id="name" name="name" required>
   </div>
   <div class="form-field">
      <label for="email">Your Email</label>
      <input type="email" id="email" name="email" required>
   </div>
   <div class="form-field">
      <label for="message">Your Message</label>
      <textarea id="message" name="message" required></textarea>
   </div>
   <button type="submit">Submit</button>
```

```
</form>

<script>
  // Function to validate the form
  function validateForm(event) {
    event.preventDefault();  // Prevent form submission

    const name = document.getElementById('name').value.trim();
    const email = document.getElementById('email').value.trim();
    const message = document.getElementById('message').value.trim();

    // Validate name
    if (name === "") {
      alert("Name is required.");
      return false;
    }

    // Validate email format using regular expression
    const emailPattern = /^[a-zA-Z0-9._-]+@[a-zA-Z0-9.-]+\.[a-zA-Z]{2,6}$/;
    if (!emailPattern.test(email)) {
      alert("Please enter a valid email address.");
      return false;
    }

    // Validate message
    if (message === "") {
      alert("Please enter a message.");
      return false;
    }
```

```
// If validation passes, submit the form (just a simulation for now)
alert("Form submitted successfully!");
return true;
}
```

```
// Attach the validateForm function to the form's submit event
document.getElementById('contactForm').addEventListener('submit',
validateForm);
</script>
```

```
</body>
</html>
```

Explanation:

1. **HTML Structure**: The contact form includes fields for the user's name, email, and message. All fields are required.

2. **CSS Styling**: Basic styling is applied to make the form look clean and easy to use.

3. **JavaScript Validation**:
   - The validateForm function checks whether the name, email, and message fields are filled correctly.
   - The email is validated using a regular expression to ensure it follows the correct format.
   - Alerts are shown if any field is invalid, and the form submission is prevented using event.preventDefault().

o If the input is valid, a success message is displayed, and the form would be submitted (in a real scenario, you'd submit the form data to a server).

In this chapter, we've learned the key concepts of **form elements** and **validation** in JavaScript. By understanding how to create and interact with form elements, as well as ensuring user input is valid, we can build robust, user-friendly web applications. In the next chapter, we'll dive deeper into **JavaScript events** and explore more advanced techniques for making your websites interactive.

CHAPTER 12: ASYNCHRONOUS JAVASCRIPT – AJAX AND FETCH

In modern web development, interactivity and real-time data updates are key to creating dynamic user experiences. **Asynchronous JavaScript** (often abbreviated as **AJAX**) is a powerful tool for making web pages responsive without needing to reload the page. This chapter will introduce you to asynchronous programming concepts and show you how to use AJAX and the modern **Fetch API** to work with external data like APIs.

---

1. Introduction to Asynchronous JavaScript

JavaScript, by default, is **synchronous**, meaning each line of code runs sequentially, and the next line doesn't execute until the current one finishes. However, web applications often need to perform time-consuming operations (like fetching data from a server or interacting with a database) without blocking the user interface.

To address this, JavaScript allows for **asynchronous operations** that let your application perform tasks in the background, enabling a smooth user experience. Asynchronous operations can happen independently of the main program flow, allowing the application to keep running without waiting for the task to complete.

Key Concepts in Asynchronous JavaScript:

1. **Event Loop**:
    o JavaScript is single-threaded, meaning it processes one operation at a time. However, the event loop enables asynchronous operations by using a **message queue** to handle tasks like waiting for network responses.
    o When an asynchronous operation (such as an API request) completes, the callback function is added to the message queue, and the event loop processes it when the main thread is free.

2. **Callbacks**:
    o A **callback** is a function passed as an argument to another function and is executed once a task is completed. However, relying heavily on callbacks can lead to **callback hell**, where multiple nested callbacks make code difficult to read and maintain.

3. **Promises**:

o **Promises** were introduced to handle asynchronous operations more efficiently. A promise represents the eventual completion (or failure) of an asynchronous operation and allows you to chain .then() methods to handle success or failure.

4. **Async/Await**:

   o With **async/await**, JavaScript introduced a more readable syntax for handling promises. It allows you to write asynchronous code as if it were synchronous, making it easier to work with.

2. AJAX (Asynchronous JavaScript and XML)

AJAX is the foundation of modern dynamic web applications. It allows the browser to send and receive data from a server asynchronously, meaning that the page doesn't need to reload to update the content.

AJAX was originally used with **XML**, but nowadays, it is more commonly used with **JSON** for data exchange due to its simplicity and efficiency.

AJAX Workflow:

1. The client (browser) sends an **HTTP request** (GET, POST, etc.) to the server.

2. The server processes the request and returns a response (typically in JSON or XML format).

3. The client processes the response and updates the webpage dynamically, without reloading.

AJAX Example:

Here's a simple example of an AJAX request using the XMLHttpRequest object, which is the older method for making AJAX requests.

javascript

```javascript
// Create a new XMLHttpRequest object
const xhr = new XMLHttpRequest();

// Define the type of request and URL
xhr.open('GET', 'https://api.example.com/data', true);

// Set up a function to handle the response
xhr.onreadystatechange = function() {
    if (xhr.readyState === 4 && xhr.status === 200) {
        const data = JSON.parse(xhr.responseText); // Parse the JSON response
        console.log(data);
    }
};

// Send the request
xhr.send();
```

While XMLHttpRequest works well, it is more cumbersome and has several limitations. The more modern **Fetch API** is simpler and more powerful.

---

3. Fetch API: Modern Asynchronous Requests

The **Fetch API** is the modern standard for making HTTP requests in JavaScript. It provides a cleaner and more flexible way to work with asynchronous requests. Unlike XMLHttpRequest, the fetch() method returns a **promise**, allowing you to use .then() or async/await to handle the response.

Basic Syntax:

javascript

```
fetch(url, options)
    .then(response => response.json())  // Convert the response to JSON
    .then(data => console.log(data))    // Handle the response data
    .catch(error => console.error('Error:', error)); // Handle errors
```

Example of a GET Request Using Fetch:

Here's how you can use the Fetch API to make a simple GET request to an API:

javascript

```
fetch('https://api.example.com/data')
    .then(response => {
        if (!response.ok) {
```

```
    throw new Error('Network response was not ok');
  }
  return response.json(); // Parse JSON from the response
})
.then(data => console.log(data)) // Handle the data
.catch(error => console.error('There was a problem with the fetch operation:',
error));
```

In this example, fetch() returns a promise that resolves with the response object. We then check if the response was successful (status code 200) and parse the response into a JavaScript object using .json(). If there's an error, the .catch() method handles it.

---

4. Real-World Example: Displaying Weather Data

In this section, we'll create a small weather app that fetches weather data from a public API and displays it on the page. For this example, we'll use the **OpenWeatherMap API**.

1. **Sign up for an API key**: Go to OpenWeatherMap and sign up to get an API key.

2. **Make the Fetch Request**: We'll make a GET request to fetch the weather data based on the user's city input.

HTML:

html

```
<!DOCTYPE html>
<html lang="en">
```

```html
<head>
   <meta charset="UTF-8">
   <meta name="viewport" content="width=device-width, initial-scale=1.0">
   <title>Weather App</title>
   <style>
      body { font-family: Arial, sans-serif; margin: 20px; }
      input { padding: 8px; font-size: 16px; }
      button { padding: 10px 20px; background-color: #4CAF50; color: white;
border: none; cursor: pointer; }
      .weather-info { margin-top: 20px; }
   </style>
</head>
<body>

<h1>Weather App</h1>
<p>Enter a city name to get the current weather:</p>
<input type="text" id="city" placeholder="Enter city">
<button onclick="getWeather()">Get Weather</button>

<div class="weather-info" id="weather-info"></div>

<script src="script.js"></script>
</body>
</html>
```

JavaScript (script.js):

javascript

```javascript
function getWeather() {
   const city = document.getElementById('city').value;
   const apiKey = 'your-api-key'; // Replace with your API key
```

```
const                          url                          =
`https://api.openweathermap.org/data/2.5/weather?q=${city}&appid=${apiKey}
&units=metric`;

  fetch(url)
    .then(response => {
      if (!response.ok) {
        throw new Error('City not found');
      }
      return response.json();
    })
    .then(data => {
      const weather = `
        <h2>Weather in ${data.name}</h2>
        <p>Temperature: ${data.main.temp}°C</p>
        <p>Weather: ${data.weather[0].description}</p>
        <p>Humidity: ${data.main.humidity}%</p>
      `;
      document.getElementById('weather-info').innerHTML = weather;
    })
    .catch(error => {
      document.getElementById('weather-info').innerHTML    =    `<p>Error:
${error.message}</p>`;
    });
}
```

Explanation:

1. The user enters a city name, and when they click the "Get Weather" button, the getWeather() function is triggered.

2. Inside getWeather(), we make a **fetch** request to the OpenWeatherMap API, passing the city and API key in the URL.

3. The **response** is parsed as JSON, and we extract the temperature, weather description, and humidity.

4. The weather information is displayed dynamically on the page.

5. If there's an error (e.g., the city isn't found), we catch it and display an error message.

In this chapter, we've learned how to use **asynchronous JavaScript** techniques like **AJAX** and the **Fetch API** to work with data from external sources. We saw how asynchronous programming allows web applications to stay responsive while waiting for tasks like fetching data. By using fetch(), we can easily make HTTP requests, handle responses, and update the page dynamically, creating more interactive and real-time user experiences. In the next chapter, we'll dive deeper into **advanced JavaScript concepts**, including error handling and performance optimization techniques.

CHAPTER 13: INTRODUCTION TO RESPONSIVE DESIGN

As web development has evolved, so have the devices we use to browse the web. From desktop computers to smartphones, tablets, and wearables, users now access websites on a variety of screen sizes and resolutions. This shift has made **responsive design** a critical part of web development. In this chapter, we'll explore what responsive design is, how to implement it using **CSS media queries**, and how to handle different screen sizes and devices to create a seamless user experience across all platforms.

---

1. What is Responsive Design?

Responsive Web Design (RWD) refers to the practice of designing web pages that automatically adjust and adapt to the size of the screen on which they are being viewed. Instead of creating separate websites or pages for each device (e.g., one for mobile, one for tablet, one for desktop), responsive design allows you to use the same codebase to deliver a customized experience for every device.

Responsive design ensures that your content is:

- **Accessible**: Users can read and navigate the site easily, regardless of device.
- **Efficient**: Developers only need to create one version of the website, making maintenance easier.
- **User-Friendly**: The layout and features of the site will adjust for the most optimal viewing experience.

Core Principles of Responsive Design:

1. **Fluid Layouts**: Use percentage-based widths, rather than fixed pixel widths, so the layout can adapt to different screen sizes.
2. **Flexible Images**: Images should scale and resize based on the screen size to prevent them from breaking the layout.
3. **Media Queries**: Apply different CSS rules depending on the device's characteristics, such as screen width or resolution.
4. **Mobile-First Design**: Start by designing for small screens (mobile devices) and gradually scale up, adding complexity as the screen size increases.

2. Media Queries: Adapting Styles to Different Devices

CSS media queries are a powerful feature that allow you to apply styles depending on specific conditions like screen width, resolution, or orientation. This is the cornerstone of responsive design because it enables the application of different styling rules based on the device characteristics.

Basic Syntax of Media Queries:

css

```
@media (condition) {
  /* CSS rules to apply when the condition is true */
}
```

- **Condition** can include a variety of device features like width, height, orientation, and resolution.

For example:

css

```
/* Default styles */
body {
    font-size: 16px;
}

/* Styles for devices with a width of 600px or less (e.g., mobile phones) */
@media (max-width: 600px) {
```

```
body {
    font-size: 14px;
  }
}


/* Styles for tablets with a width between 600px and 1024px */
@media (min-width: 600px) and (max-width: 1024px) {
  body {
    font-size: 15px;
  }
}


/* Styles for large screens (desktops) */
@media (min-width: 1024px) {
  body {
    font-size: 18px;
  }
}
```

In the example above:

- For small screens (like smartphones), the body font size is set to 14px.
- For tablets, it's adjusted to 15px.
- For larger screens, like desktops, the font size becomes 18px.

Common Media Queries:

1. **Max-width**: Targets screens with a maximum width (e.g., for mobile or tablet views).

   css

   @media (max-width: 768px) { /* CSS for small screens */ }

2. **Min-width**: Targets screens with a minimum width (e.g., for larger screens or desktops).

   css

   @media (min-width: 1024px) { /* CSS for large screens */ }

3. **Orientation**: Targets the device's orientation (portrait or landscape).

   css

   @media (orientation: portrait) { /* CSS for portrait orientation */ }

By using these queries, we can modify the layout, font sizes, images, and other elements to suit the user's screen size.

---

3. Viewport and Units: Designing for Flexibility

When designing for various screen sizes, it's important to understand how the browser renders the page and scales elements. The **viewport** is the visible area of the web page on the screen. By controlling the viewport and choosing the right units, you can ensure that your page looks great on any device.

Viewport Meta Tag:

The viewport meta tag allows you to control the scaling and width of the page on mobile devices, ensuring that it displays at the right size.

html

```html
<meta name="viewport" content="width=device-width, initial-scale=1">
```

- **width=device-width**: Sets the width of the viewport to the width of the device screen.
- **initial-scale=1**: Sets the initial zoom level (1 means no zoom).

This tag is essential for making a webpage responsive on mobile devices.

Responsive Units:

To create fluid layouts, it's essential to use responsive units that scale according to the screen size.

1. **Viewport Width (vw)**: 1vw is equal to 1% of the viewport's width.

   css

width: 50vw; /* 50% of the viewport width */

2. **Viewport Height (vh)**: 1vh is equal to 1% of the viewport's height.

css

height: 100vh; /* 100% of the viewport height */

3. **Percentage (%)**: The percentage unit is relative to the parent element's size. It's useful for creating flexible containers.

css

width: 50%; /* 50% of the parent element's width */

4. **em and rem**:
   - **em**: Relative to the font-size of the parent element.
   - **rem**: Relative to the root element's font-size (typically <html>).

Using these units, elements can scale based on the size of the viewport, making the layout more adaptable.

4. Real-World Example: Creating a Webpage for Multiple Devices

Let's create a simple webpage that adjusts for mobile, tablet, and desktop views. We'll use the concepts of **media queries**, the **viewport meta tag**, and **responsive units** to design the layout.

HTML:

html

```html
<!DOCTYPE html>
<html lang="en">
<head>
  <meta charset="UTF-8">
  <meta name="viewport" content="width=device-width, initial-scale=1">
  <title>Responsive Web Page</title>
  <link rel="stylesheet" href="styles.css">
</head>
<body>

<header>
  <h1>Responsive Design Example</h1>
  <nav>
    <ul>
      <li><a href="#">Home</a></li>
      <li><a href="#">About</a></li>
      <li><a href="#">Services</a></li>
      <li><a href="#">Contact</a></li>
    </ul>
  </nav>
</header>

<section class="content">
```

```html
<h2>Responsive Layout</h2>
<p>This layout adapts to different screen sizes using media queries and flexible units.</p>
</section>

<footer>
<p>&copy; 2024 Responsive Web Design</p>
</footer>

</body>
</html>
```

CSS (styles.css):

css

```css
/* Basic Styling */
body {
    font-family: Arial, sans-serif;
    margin: 0;
    padding: 0;
}

header {
    background-color: #333;
    color: white;
    padding: 20px;
    text-align: center;
}

nav ul {
    list-style-type: none;
```

```css
   padding: 0;
}

nav ul li {
   display: inline-block;
   margin-right: 20px;
}

nav ul li a {
   color: white;
   text-decoration: none;
}

section.content {
   padding: 20px;
}

footer {
   background-color: #333;
   color: white;
   text-align: center;
   padding: 10px;
}

/* Media Queries for Mobile Devices */
@media (max-width: 600px) {
   header {
      text-align: left;
   }
```

```css
  nav ul {
    text-align: center;
  }

  nav ul li {
    display: block;
    margin-bottom: 10px;
  }
}

/* Media Queries for Tablets */
@media (min-width: 601px) and (max-width: 1024px) {
  nav ul li {
    display: inline-block;
    margin-right: 15px;
  }

  header {
    text-align: center;
  }
}

/* Media Queries for Desktops */
@media (min-width: 1025px) {
  header {
    text-align: center;
  }

  nav ul li {
    display: inline-block;
```

```
    margin-right: 25px;
  }
}
```

Explanation:

1. **Viewport Meta Tag**: Ensures proper scaling on mobile devices.

2. **CSS Layout**: Basic styles set for header, navigation, content, and footer.

3. **Media Queries**:

    o **For mobile** (max-width: 600px), the header text aligns to the left, and navigation links are stacked vertically.

    o **For tablets** (601px to 1024px), the navigation links are aligned horizontally, and the header remains centered.

    o **For desktops** (1025px and above), the header and navigation are laid out for larger screens, with more spacing between items.

This layout adjusts dynamically based on the screen size, ensuring that it looks good on mobile, tablet, and desktop devices.

Responsive design is essential for ensuring that your websites are accessible and user-friendly across all devices. By using **media queries**, **flexible units** (like vw, vh, %), and **viewport control**, you can create fluid layouts that adjust to different screen sizes and resolutions. This approach not only improves the user experience but also makes your development process more efficient, as you only need to maintain a single codebase for all devices. In the next chapter, we'll explore how to take your responsive designs further by diving deeper into **CSS Grid** and **Flexbox** for even more advanced layouts.

CHAPTER 14: MOBILE-FIRST DESIGN

In the modern web development landscape, designing for mobile devices first is no longer a trend—it's a necessity. With the majority of global web traffic coming from smartphones and mobile devices, **mobile-first design** has become a foundational principle of creating responsive and user-friendly websites. In this chapter, we'll dive into the **principles of mobile-first design**, discuss **progressive enhancement** as a strategy, and walk through a **real-world example** of building a mobile-first landing page.

---

1. Principles of Mobile-First Design

Mobile-first design refers to the practice of designing websites starting with the smallest screen size in mind, then progressively enhancing the design for larger screens. This approach places a heavy emphasis on **usability, performance, and simplicity** by optimizing the user experience for mobile devices first and then building upon that for desktops and tablets.

Why Start with the Smallest Screen Size?

1. **Focus on Essential Content**: Mobile screens have limited real estate, so designing for the smallest screen forces you to prioritize essential content and functionality. This encourages cleaner, simpler designs and ensures that the most important elements are front and center.

2. **Faster Load Times**: Mobile-first design ensures that mobile users get a lightweight, faster-loading version of the site. By starting small, you can minimize resources (like large images and complex scripts) that may slow down the experience on mobile devices.

3. **User-Centered Design**: Mobile-first places the **user experience** at the core of the design process. Mobile users typically want quick access to key actions, such as scrolling, tapping, and navigating without clutter. Designing with this in mind allows you to create intuitive and easy-to-use interfaces.

4. **Better for SEO**: Google uses mobile-first indexing, meaning the mobile version of your website is considered the primary version. Starting with mobile helps ensure better search engine ranking and visibility for mobile users.

5. **Adapting to the Future**: As mobile technology continues to dominate, mobile-first design ensures that your site is adaptable to future devices that will continue to innovate with smaller and more varied screen sizes.

Core Aspects of Mobile-First Design:

- **Prioritize Content**: Start by displaying only the essential information and functionality for mobile devices, ensuring a clean and efficient experience.

- **Optimize Performance**: Minimize heavy assets such as large images and videos, as they can slow down mobile browsing.

- **Responsive Layouts**: Use flexible units like percentages and viewport-based units (vw, vh) to ensure elements scale smoothly on various screen sizes.

- **Touch-Friendly Elements**: Mobile users interact with their devices using their fingers, so it's important to design with touch interactions in mind (e.g., bigger buttons, swipeable elements).

2. Progressive Enhancement

While mobile-first design focuses on creating a great experience for mobile users first, **progressive enhancement** is the strategy of building a baseline experience for all users and then adding more advanced features and functionality for users with better devices or higher screen resolutions.

What is Progressive Enhancement?

Progressive enhancement ensures that your website works for all users, regardless of the technology they use. It starts with a basic, functional layout and then adds more advanced styling and features as the screen size, browser capabilities, and device performance increase.

How It Works:

- **Start Simple**: Begin by building a basic structure for your website that works well on mobile devices. This means minimal styling and essential content.
- **Add Layers for Larger Screens**: Once the mobile design is in place, use CSS media queries to progressively enhance the design for larger screens. Add more complex layouts, interactions, and richer content as the screen space grows.
- **Optimize for Performance**: Even on desktop, ensure that the site is optimized for performance. For example, images can load in higher resolution only on larger screens.

- **Backward Compatibility**: It ensures that users with older browsers or devices can still access your content, even if it doesn't feature all the bells and whistles.
- **Improved Accessibility**: By starting with a simple, functional layout, you make your website more accessible to people who may rely on basic browsers or assistive technology.
- **Scalability**: The design grows and adapts based on the device's capabilities, which helps future-proof your website.

---

3. Real-World Example: Building a Mobile-First Landing Page

Let's go through a simple example of building a **mobile-first landing page** that focuses on clean, essential content and progressively enhances it for larger screens. We'll use **responsive images** and **typography** to ensure a smooth experience across all devices.

HTML Structure (index.html):

html

```
<!DOCTYPE html>
<html lang="en">
<head>
  <meta charset="UTF-8">
```

```
<meta name="viewport" content="width=device-width, initial-scale=1">
<title>Mobile-First Landing Page</title>
<link rel="stylesheet" href="styles.css">
</head>
<body>

<header>
  <h1>Welcome to Our Service</h1>
  <p>Your go-to solution for all things web development.</p>
  <button id="cta-button">Get Started</button>
</header>

<section class="features">
  <div class="feature-item">
    <h2>Fast and Reliable</h2>
    <p>Experience the speed and reliability that our platform offers.</p>
  </div>
  <div class="feature-item">
    <h2>Secure and Safe</h2>
    <p>Your data is always protected with top-notch security features.</p>
  </div>
</section>

<footer>
  <p>&copy; 2024 Mobile-First Landing Page</p>
</footer>

</body>
</html>
```

CSS (styles.css):

css

```css
/* Base Styles (for mobile devices) */
body {
    font-family: Arial, sans-serif;
    margin: 0;
    padding: 0;
    background-color: #f4f4f4;
}

header {
    text-align: center;
    padding: 20px;
    background-color: #007bff;
    color: white;
}

h1 {
    font-size: 24px;
}

button {
    padding: 10px 20px;
    font-size: 16px;
    background-color: #28a745;
    border: none;
    color: white;
    cursor: pointer;
}
```

```css
/* Layout for features section */
.features {
    display: flex;
    flex-direction: column;
    padding: 20px;
}

.feature-item {
    background-color: #fff;
    margin: 10px 0;
    padding: 15px;
    border-radius: 5px;
    box-shadow: 0 2px 4px rgba(0, 0, 0, 0.1);
}

/* Media Queries for Tablets */
@media (min-width: 600px) {
    header {
        padding: 30px;
    }

    h1 {
        font-size: 32px;
    }

    .features {
        flex-direction: row;
        justify-content: space-around;
    }
}
```

```css
.feature-item {
    width: 45%;
  }
}

/* Media Queries for Desktops */
@media (min-width: 1024px) {
  header {
    padding: 40px;
  }

  h1 {
    font-size: 36px;
  }

  .feature-item {
    width: 30%;
  }
}
```

Explanation:

- **Mobile-First Base Styles**: The layout starts with a simple header, a call-to-action button, and a stacked features section (column layout). These styles are designed for small screen sizes (mobile-first).

- **Progressive Enhancement with Media Queries**:

- o For **tablets** (min-width: 600px), the layout changes to a horizontal arrangement, with the two feature items side by side.
- o For **desktops** (min-width: 1024px), the text size and padding are further enhanced, and the feature items are resized to take up 30% of the width, allowing for a more spacious layout.

- **Responsive Images**: While not shown in the CSS above, you would use the <picture> element or srcset in the <img> tag to load different image sizes based on the screen width. For example:

html

```
<img src="image-small.jpg" srcset="image-large.jpg 1024w, image-medium.jpg 600w" alt="Feature Image">
```

This example ensures that the landing page looks clean and functional on mobile devices while progressively enhancing the design for tablets and desktops.

Mobile-first design isn't just a best practice—it's a necessity for building modern, responsive websites that offer an excellent user experience. By starting with the smallest screen and progressively enhancing your design, you can ensure that your website is accessible, functional, and optimized for any device. The principles of **mobile-first design** and **progressive enhancement** help create scalable and adaptive websites that look great on any screen, from mobile phones to desktop monitors.

In the next chapter, we'll take a deeper dive into more advanced CSS layout techniques using **CSS Grid** and **Flexbox**, further expanding your responsive design toolkit.

CHAPTER 15: DEBUGGING AND TESTING FRONT-END CODE

Debugging and testing are critical steps in the web development process, helping ensure that websites are functional, efficient, and user-friendly. In this chapter, we'll cover the essential tools and techniques for debugging and testing front-end code, specifically focusing on **browser developer tools**, common **issues and fixes**, and how to **unit test** JavaScript with libraries like **Jest**. We will also walk through a **real-world example** of debugging a website with layout and functionality issues.

1. Browser Developer Tools

Modern web browsers come with built-in **developer tools** that are essential for debugging HTML, CSS, and JavaScript directly in the browser. These tools provide an interactive way to inspect elements, test functionality, and fix issues without having to make constant changes in your code editor.

Key Features of Browser Developer Tools:

1. **Elements Panel (HTML and CSS)**: This allows you to view and modify the HTML structure and CSS styling of your page. You can:

   o Inspect elements on the page by right-clicking and selecting **Inspect**.

   o Edit the HTML structure, including adding, removing, or changing tags.

   o Modify the CSS rules in real-time and see the changes immediately.

   o Check box models and margins/paddings to troubleshoot layout issues.

   Tip: Use the **Computed** tab to view the final values of all styles applied to an element.

2. **Console Panel (JavaScript Debugging)**: The **Console** tab is where you can view logged output, error messages, and run JavaScript commands.

   o Use console.log() in your code to display values or debug errors.

   o The **Errors** section helps you identify JavaScript errors and provides stack traces, which point to the exact line causing the issue.

3. **Network Panel**: This shows all the network requests made by your webpage, including APIs, images, scripts, and stylesheets. It is crucial for debugging issues related to missing or failed resources, slow-loading files, or incorrect API responses.

4. **Performance and Memory Panels**: These tools help diagnose performance bottlenecks and memory leaks. They allow you to track page load times, measure JavaScript execution, and identify areas that can be optimized.

Real-Time Debugging Example:

If a button on your page isn't working, right-click and inspect it in the **Elements** panel to check if it has the correct event listeners. You can also check for any errors in the **Console** related to that button's functionality. If the button's styling is incorrect, check the **CSS** in the **Styles** pane to see which styles are overriding it.

2. Common Issues and Fixes

Front-end developers often face a wide range of issues. Here are some common problems and how to solve them:

Layout Issues:

- **Problem**: Elements are not aligning correctly (e.g., buttons appearing out of place, images overlapping).
- **Solution**: Check if the container elements have proper width, padding, and margin values. Use **Flexbox** or **CSS Grid** for better layout control. In the **Elements** tab, check the **box model** to see if any margins, padding, or border properties are causing the misalignment.

Broken JavaScript:

- **Problem**: Scripts fail to run or throw errors (e.g., undefined variables, missing functions).
- **Solution**: Open the **Console** panel to check for any error messages. Look at the error stack trace to pinpoint the line causing the issue. Make sure that JavaScript files are correctly linked in your HTML, and that functions or variables are correctly defined.

Browser Compatibility:

- **Problem**: The website works in one browser but looks broken in another (e.g., layout issues, missing styles, or JavaScript errors).
- **Solution**: Test your site in multiple browsers (e.g., Chrome, Firefox, Safari, Edge) to identify discrepancies. Use **Autoprefixer** or **CSS vendor prefixes** to ensure compatibility with different browsers. For JavaScript, consider **polyfills** or **feature detection** libraries like **Modernizr**.

Responsive Design Issues:

- **Problem**: The website looks fine on desktop but breaks on smaller screens (e.g., images not resizing, text overlapping).
- **Solution**: Check your **media queries** to ensure they are targeting the correct breakpoints. Use the **device toolbar** in the developer tools to simulate different screen sizes and make necessary adjustments to the CSS.

---

3. Unit Testing in JavaScript

Testing your JavaScript code helps ensure that it behaves as expected and is free from errors. One of the most popular libraries for writing and running unit tests is **Jest**.

What is Unit Testing?

Unit testing is the practice of testing individual units or components of your code (usually functions) to verify that they work correctly in isolation. For front-end developers, unit testing is particularly useful for JavaScript logic, including form validation, event handling, and API calls.

Getting Started with Jest:

1. **Installation**: First, install Jest using npm (Node Package Manager):

bash

npm install --save-dev jest

2. **Writing Tests**: Create a test file (e.g., app.test.js) and write your tests using Jest's built-in methods. Here's a simple test for a function that calculates the area of a rectangle:

javascript

```
// area.js
function calculateArea(width, height) {
    return width * height;
}

module.exports = calculateArea;
```
javascript

```
// area.test.js
const calculateArea = require('./area');

test('calculates the area of a rectangle correctly', () => {
    expect(calculateArea(5, 10)).toBe(50);
    expect(calculateArea(7, 3)).toBe(21);
});
```

3. **Running Tests**: Run your tests by executing the following command in the terminal:

   bash

   npm test

   Jest will run all the test cases and provide a summary of which tests passed or failed.

Mocking Functions and APIs:

In many cases, you'll need to test functions that rely on external services (e.g., API calls). Jest provides built-in support for **mocking** functions, which allows you to simulate external services and control their behavior during testing.

Example of mocking a fetch request:

javascript

```
jest.mock('node-fetch');
const fetch = require('node-fetch');
const { Response } = jest.requireActual('node-fetch');
```

```
// Mock the API response
fetch.mockResolvedValue(new Response(JSON.stringify({ data: 'test' }), {
status: 200 }));
```

4. Real-World Example: Debugging a Website's Layout and Functionality

Imagine you are working on a project for a client, and their website's **layout is broken** on mobile devices, and **JavaScript functionality** isn't working correctly (e.g., a button that doesn't show a modal). Here's how you would approach the issue:

Step 1: Use Browser Developer Tools

- **Inspect the Layout**: Open the browser's developer tools and check the HTML and CSS of the affected sections. Identify any problematic styles or missing CSS rules.

- **Check the Console for Errors**: Open the Console tab to look for JavaScript errors. Let's say you see an error like Uncaught TypeError: Cannot read property 'addEventListener' of null. This indicates that the JavaScript is trying to attach an event listener to an element that doesn't exist in the DOM.

Step 2: Identify and Fix the Issues

- **CSS Fix**: If the layout issue is due to missing styles for mobile screens, add the necessary **media queries** and make sure the elements are correctly responsive.

- **JavaScript Fix**: If the button issue is due to an incorrect selector, check the DOM for the correct element ID or class name. Ensure the script is being loaded after the DOM is ready (using window.onload or placing scripts at the end of the body tag).

Step 3: Test the Fix

After making the fixes, re-test the website in multiple browsers and screen sizes using the developer tools. Make sure the layout is working as expected and that the JavaScript functionality (e.g., the button clicking) is now working properly.

Step 4: Unit Test the JavaScript

Once the functionality is fixed, write a unit test for the JavaScript functionality to ensure it works as expected in the future. For example, test the button's event listener functionality and any related business logic.

Effective debugging and testing are essential skills for front-end developers to ensure that websites function properly across all browsers and devices. **Browser developer tools** are invaluable for inspecting, debugging, and improving your code in real-time. By understanding common issues and employing strategies such as **unit testing** with tools like **Jest**, you can create reliable, performant websites. Debugging and testing are iterative processes, and by using these tools and techniques, you'll be able to handle even the most challenging issues with confidence.

CHAPTER 16: INTRODUCTION TO VERSION CONTROL – GIT AND GITHUB

Version control is a critical tool in modern web development, allowing developers to manage changes to their codebase, collaborate effectively with others, and track project history. In this chapter, we will explore **Git**, a powerful distributed version control system, and **GitHub**, a platform for hosting Git repositories and enabling collaboration. You will learn the core concepts of version control, the most common Git commands, and how to leverage GitHub for efficient teamwork. We'll also walk through a **real-world example** of setting up a Git repository for a web development project and collaborating with others.

---

1. What is Git?

Git is a **distributed version control system (VCS)** that allows multiple developers to work on the same project concurrently without interfering with each other's changes. Unlike centralized version control systems, Git gives every developer a full copy of the repository, enabling them to work offline and sync with the central repository when ready.

Why Use Git in Front-End Development?

- **Track Changes**: Git helps you keep track of all changes made to your project, whether it's an HTML file, a CSS stylesheet, or JavaScript code. Every time a change is made, Git records it as a "commit," allowing you to go back in time and restore previous versions if necessary.
- **Collaboration**: In a team setting, Git allows developers to work in parallel, merging their changes safely. It helps prevent conflicts, and in case they occur, Git offers tools to resolve them.

- **Backup**: By using remote repositories, Git offers a cloud-based backup of your code, ensuring your work is safe even if your local machine is lost or damaged.

Key Concepts in Git:

- **Repository (Repo)**: A Git repository is a project directory where Git tracks all changes. It can be either local (on your computer) or remote (on a platform like GitHub).
- **Commit**: A commit is a snapshot of your project at a particular point in time. It includes a message explaining the changes made.
- **Branch**: A branch is an isolated environment where developers can work on new features or fixes without affecting the main codebase (usually called main or master).
- **Merge**: Merging combines changes from different branches into one. If there are conflicts between changes, Git will ask you to resolve them.

---

2. Basic Git Commands

To begin using Git, you need to familiarize yourself with a few essential commands. Below are the most common Git commands and their functions:

Cloning a Repository

To start working on an existing Git repository (e.g., one hosted on GitHub), you first need to clone it to your local machine.

bash

git clone https://github.com/username/repository.git

This command creates a copy of the repository on your local machine, and you can begin making changes.

Creating a Branch

Once you have a repository on your local machine, you can create a new branch to work on without affecting the main project.

bash

git checkout -b new-feature

This creates and switches to a new branch called new-feature. You can now make changes specific to that feature.

Making Changes and Committing

After making changes to the code (e.g., adding a new HTML page, updating a CSS file, or fixing a JavaScript bug), you need to save them to Git.

1. **Stage Changes**: This tells Git which changes you want to include in your next commit.

   bash

git add .

This command stages all the changes in the current directory. Alternatively, you can specify individual files instead of . (e.g., git add index.html).

2. **Commit Changes**: After staging the changes, you commit them to your local repository with a message.

bash

git commit -m "Added new feature"

Always write clear, concise commit messages that describe the changes you've made. This helps collaborators understand the purpose of the commit.

Pushing Changes to GitHub

Once you're satisfied with your changes and have committed them locally, you can push them to a remote repository (e.g., GitHub) to share them with others.

bash

git push origin new-feature

This command pushes the new-feature branch to GitHub. If you're pushing to the main branch, replace new-feature with main.

Pulling Changes from GitHub

If you're collaborating with others, you need to keep your local repository updated with the latest changes made by your teammates. Use the following command to pull the latest changes from GitHub:

bash

git pull origin main

This will fetch and merge changes from the main branch on GitHub into your local main branch.

Merging Branches

Once your feature is complete and you've tested it locally, you need to merge it back into the main branch. First, switch to the main branch:

bash

git checkout main

Then, merge the changes from your feature branch:

bash

git merge new-feature

If there are no conflicts, Git will merge the changes automatically. If there are conflicts, you'll need to resolve them manually.

---

3. GitHub for Collaboration

GitHub is an online platform that hosts Git repositories, enabling easy collaboration among developers. With GitHub, multiple developers can work on the same project simultaneously, track changes, and even review code before merging it into the main project.

Creating a Repository on GitHub

1. **Create a New Repository**: Go to your GitHub profile, click the **New** button, and fill in the repository details.
2. **Push Local Changes to GitHub**: Once you have made your local commits and are ready to share them, you can push your changes to your GitHub repository using the git push command as mentioned earlier.

Pull Requests (PRs)

Pull requests are used to propose changes from one branch to another (often from a feature branch to the main branch). They are an essential tool for code reviews and collaboration.

1. **Create a Pull Request**: On GitHub, navigate to your repository and click **New Pull Request**. Select the branch you want to merge into main (usually your feature branch) and submit the PR.
2. **Review and Discuss**: Team members can review the changes, leave comments, and suggest improvements.
3. **Merge the Pull Request**: Once the PR is approved, it can be merged into the main branch, making the changes part of the project.

1. **Forking**: If you are contributing to someone else's project, you can **fork** the repository, create your own branches, and submit pull requests with your changes.

2. **Issues**: GitHub allows users to open **issues** for bug reports, feature requests, or discussions, which helps organize tasks and track progress.

3. **GitHub Actions**: You can automate various workflows using **GitHub Actions**, such as running tests, building your project, or deploying it to production.

---

4. Real-World Example: Setting Up a Git Repository for Your Web Development Project

Imagine you're working on a **web development project** for a portfolio website. You're using Git and GitHub to manage your codebase and collaborate with a team of developers. Here's how you can set up and use Git for this project:

Step 1: Initialize Your Git Repository

First, create a directory for your project:

bash

```
mkdir portfolio-website
cd portfolio-website
```

Then, initialize Git:

bash

git init

This command turns your project folder into a Git repository.

Step 2: Create a Repository on GitHub

1. Go to GitHub, log in, and create a new repository named **portfolio-website**.
2. After creating the repository, GitHub will show you instructions for linking your local repository to the remote one. Follow these commands:

   bash

   ```
   git remote add origin https://github.com/username/portfolio-website.git
   git branch -M main
   git push -u origin main
   ```

Step 3: Make Changes and Commit

You begin working on the website, making changes to the HTML, CSS, and JavaScript files. After making changes, you use the following commands to stage and commit your changes:

bash

```
git add .
git commit -m "Initial commit with basic structure"
```

Step 4: Push to GitHub

Once your initial changes are committed locally, you push them to GitHub:

bash

```
git push origin main
```

Your code is now hosted on GitHub, and you can continue making changes and pushing updates as you work.

Step 5: Collaborate Using GitHub

You decide to add a new feature (e.g., a contact form) to the portfolio site. To avoid affecting the main branch, you create a new branch:

bash

```
git checkout -b contact-form
```

You work on the contact form, make changes, and commit them:

bash

```
git add .
git commit -m "Added contact form"
```

Then, push your branch to GitHub:

bash

```
git push origin contact-form
```

On GitHub, create a **Pull Request** from contact-form to main. Your teammate reviews the code, and once it's approved, you merge the pull request.

In this chapter, you've learned how to use **Git** and **GitHub** to manage your code, track changes, and collaborate effectively on front-end web development projects. With Git, you can easily revert changes, work on different features without conflicts, and ensure the integrity of your codebase. **GitHub** provides a powerful platform for hosting and collaborating on projects, making it an essential tool for both solo developers and teams. By mastering Git and GitHub, you'll streamline your development workflow, improve code quality, and enhance collaboration with other developers.

CHAPTER 17: MODERN FRONT-END TOOLS AND FRAMEWORKS

As front-end development continues to evolve, a variety of tools and frameworks have emerged to make the process faster, more efficient, and scalable. In this chapter, we will dive into the **modern front-end development tools** and frameworks, focusing on how they help streamline workflows, improve productivity, and enhance the development process. We'll cover **React**, **Vue**, and **Angular**—the most popular front-end frameworks today—as well as **build tools**, **task runners**, and **package managers** that are essential to modern web development.

By the end of this chapter, you'll have a solid understanding of the front-end tools and frameworks that dominate the industry and how to integrate them into your development workflow. We will also walk through a **real-world example** of setting up a project using **React** with **Create React App**.

---

1. Introduction to Front-End Frameworks

Front-end frameworks provide ready-to-use libraries and components that help developers build interactive and dynamic user interfaces (UIs) more efficiently. Unlike plain HTML, CSS, and JavaScript, frameworks provide structured ways to build applications that are scalable, maintainable, and easier to work with, especially in larger projects.

Popular Front-End Frameworks:

- **React**:
  - **Overview**: React is a JavaScript library for building user interfaces, primarily used for building single-page applications (SPAs). Developed and maintained by Facebook, React focuses on building

components—self-contained, reusable pieces of UI that manage their own state.

o **Core Features**:

- **Component-Based Architecture**: React applications are built from reusable components that manage their own state and render UI based on that state.

- **Virtual DOM**: React uses a virtual DOM to efficiently update the user interface. Instead of manipulating the entire DOM, React only updates the parts that need to change, which improves performance.

- **JSX**: JSX is a syntax extension that allows you to write HTML-like code directly in JavaScript files, making it easier to define UI elements and their behavior.

- **Vue**:

o **Overview**: Vue.js is a progressive JavaScript framework for building UIs. Unlike React and Angular, Vue can be incrementally adopted, meaning you can use it for smaller features within an existing project or build entire applications from the ground up.

o **Core Features**:

- **Two-Way Data Binding**: Vue offers two-way data binding, where changes in the UI are reflected in the underlying data model and vice versa.

- **Component System**: Like React, Vue uses components, but it also offers more flexibility in defining them.

- **Vue Router** and **Vuex**: For more complex applications, Vue provides built-in solutions for routing (Vue Router) and state management (Vuex).

- **Angular**:

  - **Overview**: Angular is a full-fledged front-end framework developed by Google for building complex web applications. It's a **complete solution** for building dynamic single-page applications (SPAs), providing everything from routing and state management to testing and dependency injection.

  - **Core Features**:

    - **Two-Way Data Binding**: Similar to Vue, Angular provides two-way data binding, which simplifies managing the flow of data between the UI and the app's model.

- **Directives**: Angular uses directives to extend HTML with custom tags and attributes that can manipulate the DOM.
- **Dependency Injection**: Angular's dependency injection system makes it easier to manage services and components, improving modularity and testability.

Choosing the Right Framework

- **React** is often the best choice for dynamic, component-driven applications, especially SPAs. It's lightweight, flexible, and works well for large-scale apps.
- **Vue** offers a more straightforward learning curve and is ideal for smaller projects or for developers who need gradual adoption of advanced features.
- **Angular** is suitable for enterprise-level applications that require a comprehensive, opinionated framework with all features baked in, such as routing, state management, and testing.

2. Build Tools and Task Runners

Build tools and task runners help automate repetitive development tasks, such as minification, transpiling, and bundling JavaScript, CSS, and other assets. By incorporating these tools into your workflow, you can focus more on writing code and less on managing the infrastructure of your application.

Webpack:

- **Overview**: Webpack is a popular module bundler used to bundle JavaScript files, images, and styles into a single, optimized file or several files for faster loading. It allows you to split code into **chunks** for **lazy loading** and provides various optimizations to improve performance.
- **How it Works**: Webpack uses **loaders** to transform files (like Sass into CSS or JSX into JavaScript) and **plugins** to optimize, minimize, and enhance the build process (e.g., minification, code splitting).
- **Real-World Example**: A typical Webpack configuration may look something like this:

js

```
module.exports = {
  entry: './src/index.js',
  output: {
    filename: 'bundle.js',
    path: __dirname + '/dist'
  },
  module: {
    rules: [
      {
```

```
   test: /\.js$/,
   exclude: /node_modules/,
   use: 'babel-loader'
  }
 ]
 }
};
```

Babel:

- **Overview**: Babel is a JavaScript transpiler that allows you to write modern JavaScript (ES6, ES7, JSX, etc.) and have it converted into backwards-compatible JavaScript code that runs on older browsers. It works alongside tools like Webpack to ensure that your JavaScript code can be used in a variety of environments.

- **Real-World Example**: With Babel, you can write code like this:

js

```
const greeting = () => {
  console.log('Hello, World!');
};
```

And Babel will transpile it into an older JavaScript version that can run in older browsers.

Task Runners (e.g., Gulp, npm scripts):

- **Overview**: Task runners like **Gulp** and **npm scripts** are tools that automate repetitive tasks in your development workflow. While Webpack handles bundling and optimization, task runners help with tasks like image compression, compiling Sass, running tests, and deploying code.

- **Real-World Example**: With npm scripts, you can define tasks in your package.json:

json

```
"scripts": {
  "build": "webpack --config webpack.config.js",
  "start": "webpack-dev-server --open"
}
```

3. Package Managers

Package managers like **npm** and **Yarn** help you manage dependencies in your projects. These tools allow you to install, update, and remove libraries and packages that you need for your front-end development projects.

npm (Node Package Manager):

- **Overview**: npm is the default package manager for JavaScript, which comes bundled with Node.js. It allows you to install libraries and tools, such as React, Vue, Webpack, and more, from the **npm registry**.

- **Installing Packages**: You can install packages globally or locally using commands like:

bash

npm install react
npm install --save-dev webpack

The --save-dev flag is used to install packages as **development dependencies** (e.g., build tools, testing frameworks).

Yarn:

- **Overview**: Yarn is an alternative to npm that is known for its speed, reliability, and offline support. Yarn caches every package it downloads, making subsequent installations faster. It also introduces a **lockfile** (yarn.lock) to ensure consistency across different environments.

- **Installing Packages**: Yarn has a similar syntax to npm:

bash

yarn add react
yarn add --dev webpack

Managing Dependencies:

Once you've installed your dependencies, you can track them in the package.json file. This file contains a list of all your project dependencies, both for development and production. It's crucial for sharing your project with others or deploying it to production.

---

4. Real-World Example: Setting Up a React Project Using Create React App

To understand how all these tools come together, let's walk through setting up a simple **React** project using **Create React App**—a command-line tool that helps set up a React project with a pre-configured build system, including Webpack, Babel, and npm.

Step 1: Install Node.js and npm

Before you begin, you need to have **Node.js** installed, which comes with **npm**. You can download it from the official website.

Step 2: Set Up the Project

Run the following command to create a new React application:

bash

```
npx create-react-app my-app
```

This command will generate a new folder named my-app with all the necessary files, configurations, and dependencies to start working with React.

Step 3: Start the Development Server

Navigate into the newly created project and start the development server:

bash

cd my-app
npm start

This will launch the React app on your local server at http://localhost:3000.

Step 4: Modify the App

Now, open the project in your code editor and navigate to src/App.js. Make some simple changes:

js

```js
function App() {
  return (
    <div className="App">
      <h1>Hello, React!</h1>
    </div>
  );
}
```

Save the file, and your changes will automatically reflect in the browser, thanks to the hot-reloading feature of React.

In this chapter, you learned about the modern tools and frameworks that power front-end development. We explored the essential front-end frameworks—React, Vue, and Angular—and how each framework caters to different project needs. Additionally, we covered build tools like Webpack, task runners like npm scripts, and package managers such as npm and Yarn. Finally, we walked through a **React setup** example, using **Create React App** to demonstrate how quickly you can get a project up and running with modern tools and best practices.

Mastering these tools will streamline your development process, reduce repetitive tasks, and help you build more powerful, maintainable, and scalable applications.

CHAPTER 18: WEB PERFORMANCE OPTIMIZATION

Web performance is crucial to delivering fast, smooth, and responsive user experiences. A slow website not only frustrates users but also negatively impacts search engine rankings and conversion rates. In this chapter, we will dive into essential strategies for optimizing the performance of web pages, ensuring they load quickly and run efficiently. We'll cover a range of topics, from image and asset optimization to file minification, bundling, and leveraging caching and service workers.

By the end of this chapter, you will understand how to implement performance optimization techniques and how to test and measure the performance of your web applications.

---

1. Optimizing Images and Assets

Images are often the largest assets on a webpage and can significantly impact load times. Optimizing them is one of the most effective ways to improve performance without sacrificing quality.

Image Compression

Image compression reduces the file size of images without sacrificing too much visual quality. There are two types of image compression:

- **Lossy Compression**: This reduces file size by removing some image data, resulting in a slight loss of quality. Formats like **JPEG** and **WebP** support lossy compression.
- **Lossless Compression**: This method retains all image data but reduces file size by removing unnecessary metadata and

optimizing the image format. Formats like **PNG** and **GIF** typically use lossless compression.

Tools for Image Compression:

- **TinyPNG** and **TinyJPG**: These tools automatically compress images while maintaining high visual quality.
- **ImageOptim** (Mac) or **FileOptimizer** (Windows): These are desktop tools for image optimization.
- **WebP Format**: WebP is an image format developed by Google that provides both lossy and lossless compression with better quality and smaller file sizes than PNG or JPEG. Using WebP images is a great way to optimize performance further, especially for modern browsers that support it.

Lazy Loading Images

Lazy loading defers the loading of images until they are needed, i.e., when they come into view as the user scrolls down the page. This reduces the initial page load time by loading only the images that are visible to the user.

How to Implement Lazy Loading: HTML5 has a native loading="lazy" attribute for images:

html

```
<img src="image.jpg" alt="Example Image" loading="lazy">
```

This tells the browser to only load the image when it is about to be visible in the viewport.

For greater control, you can use JavaScript-based solutions or libraries like **LazyLoad** or **IntersectionObserver**.

---

2. Minifying and Bundling Files

Minification and bundling are essential techniques for reducing file sizes and improving page load times.

Minifying CSS, JavaScript, and HTML

Minification is the process of removing unnecessary characters (such as spaces, comments, and line breaks) from your CSS, JavaScript, and HTML files. This reduces the file size, making them faster to download.

Tools for Minification:

- **CSS Minifiers**: Use tools like **cssnano** or **CleanCSS** to minify CSS files.
- **JavaScript Minifiers**: Use **Terser** or **UglifyJS** for JavaScript minification.
- **HTML Minifiers**: Tools like **HTMLMinifier** can be used to minify HTML.

Bundling Files

Bundling refers to the process of combining multiple files (CSS, JavaScript) into a single file or a few files to reduce the number of HTTP requests required to load a webpage. Fewer requests mean faster page loading and improved performance.

Tools for Bundling:

- **Webpack**: A popular JavaScript bundler, Webpack can combine your JavaScript, CSS, images, and even HTML files into a single bundle. It also allows you to use **code splitting** to load parts of your application only when needed.
- **Parcel**: A zero-config bundler that automatically handles CSS, JS, and other assets.
- **Rollup**: Another bundler that's often used for JavaScript libraries but also supports bundling of CSS and other resources.

Code Splitting: With Webpack and other modern bundlers, you can use **code splitting** to break your code into smaller chunks that are loaded as needed. This means only the essential JavaScript required for the initial page load is fetched first, and additional code is loaded as the user interacts with the site.

js

```js
// Example of code splitting in React with React.lazy
const HomePage = React.lazy(() => import('./HomePage'));
```

3. Caching and Service Workers

Caching and service workers are essential for improving performance, particularly for users with slower network connections or those accessing your website repeatedly.

Caching Techniques

Caching involves storing frequently used resources in the browser's cache to reduce loading times on subsequent visits. You can control how long files are cached by setting appropriate HTTP headers, such as Cache-Control.

Types of Caching:

- **Browser Caching**: This stores files in the user's browser so that they don't have to be re-downloaded. This can include images, CSS, JavaScript files, and even HTML.
- **Content Delivery Networks (CDNs)**: CDNs distribute copies of your files across different servers located around the world. This reduces the physical distance between your server and users, leading to faster load times.
- **HTTP Cache Headers**: Use cache-control headers to define how long a file should be cached in the browser. For example:

text

Cache-Control: max-age=31536000, immutable

This means the file will be cached for one year and won't be rechecked until that time.

Service Workers and Offline Capabilities

Service workers are JavaScript files that run in the background, separate from the web page, and allow you to cache assets and data for offline use. By intercepting network requests, service workers can serve cached assets even when the user is offline, ensuring a seamless experience.

How to Implement Service Workers: Here's a basic example of setting up a service worker:

1. Register the service worker in your main JavaScript file:

js

```js
if ('serviceWorker' in navigator) {
  navigator.serviceWorker.register('/service-worker.js')
    .then(function(registration) {
      console.log('Service Worker registered with scope:', registration.scope);
    })
    .catch(function(error) {
      console.log('Service Worker registration failed:', error);
    });
}
```

2. In your service-worker.js file, add logic to cache assets:

js

```js
self.addEventListener('install', (event) => {
  event.waitUntil(
    caches.open('my-cache').then((cache) => {
      return cache.addAll([
        '/',
        '/index.html',
        '/style.css',
        '/script.js',
      ]);
    })
  );
});

self.addEventListener('fetch', (event) => {
  event.respondWith(
    caches.match(event.request).then((response) => {
      return response || fetch(event.request);
    })
  );
});
```

Benefits of Service Workers:

- **Offline Usage**: Once assets are cached by the service worker, users can continue to use the application even when they lose internet connectivity.

- **Improved Load Time**: By serving cached content, service workers can significantly speed up the loading time of a website, particularly on repeat visits.
- **Push Notifications**: Service workers also enable features like push notifications, which can engage users even when they are not on your website.

---

4. Real-World Example: Optimizing a Website for Faster Loading

Let's take a look at a real-world example of optimizing a website for faster loading.

Imagine you are working on an e-commerce website where speed is critical for user experience and conversion rates. You decide to implement the following strategies:

1. **Optimizing Images**:
   - Compress product images using TinyPNG.
   - Convert images to the **WebP format** for browsers that support it, while providing fallback JPEGs for older browsers.
   - Implement lazy loading for product images that aren't initially visible on the page.
2. **Minifying and Bundling**:

o Minify your CSS, JavaScript, and HTML files using **Terser** and **CSSNano**.

o Bundle all JavaScript files into one file using **Webpack** and implement **code splitting** to load only the necessary JavaScript for each page.

o Use **async** and **defer** attributes on script tags to ensure non-blocking resource loading.

3. **Caching and Service Workers**:

o Implement **browser caching** for images, fonts, and static assets like CSS and JavaScript files.

o Set a long expiration time for static assets (e.g., 1 year) and shorter expiration times for dynamic content (e.g., 1 day).

o Add a **service worker** to cache key assets and enable offline usage. This allows users to browse products even when they lose internet connectivity.

o Use a **Content Delivery Network (CDN)** to serve assets from servers geographically closer to users.

4. **Final Result**:

o After implementing these optimizations, the website's page load time drops from 8 seconds to 2 seconds. The site also performs well on mobile devices and slower networks.

Web performance optimization is a crucial part of front-end development. By optimizing images, minifying and bundling files, and leveraging caching and service workers, you can significantly improve the performance of your website. These techniques lead to faster load times, better user experience, and improved search engine rankings.

By implementing these strategies and continually monitoring the performance of your website, you can create faster, more responsive web applications that keep users engaged and coming back.

CHAPTER 19: WEB ACCESSIBILITY AND SEO BASICS

In modern web development, creating an inclusive and discoverable web experience is more critical than ever. Two essential aspects of this process are **web accessibility** and **search engine optimization (SEO)**. While accessibility ensures that websites are usable by everyone, regardless of abilities or disabilities, SEO ensures that content can be easily found by search engines and users alike.

This chapter will cover the fundamental concepts of both web accessibility and SEO. We will explore the best practices for making your websites more inclusive and search-friendly, along with real-world examples that demonstrate the implementation of both.

1. What is Accessibility?

Web accessibility refers to the practice of making websites usable by people with a wide range of disabilities, including those who have visual, auditory, motor, or cognitive impairments. The goal is to ensure that all users, regardless of their abilities, can access and interact with web content without barriers.

Accessibility is not just a nice-to-have; it is a legal requirement in many countries, with accessibility guidelines such as the **Web Content Accessibility Guidelines (WCAG)** helping developers create inclusive websites.

Why Accessibility Matters

- **Inclusivity**: Accessibility ensures that websites are usable by everyone, including those with disabilities. It enables users with assistive technologies like screen readers, magnifiers, or voice control to navigate the web seamlessly.
- **Wider Audience**: Making your website accessible allows you to reach a larger audience, including people with disabilities, older users, or those with temporary impairments (e.g., a broken arm).
- **Legal Compliance**: Many countries, including the U.S. (ADA compliance), have legal frameworks that require websites to be accessible.
- **SEO Benefits**: Accessibility features often improve SEO, as search engines like Google prioritize user experience, which includes accessibility.

2. SEO Fundamentals

Search Engine Optimization (SEO) involves optimizing web content so that it ranks higher in search engine results pages (SERPs). While much of SEO is about creating valuable content, it also requires proper structuring of content and using certain technical aspects to ensure search engines can effectively crawl and index your site.

How HTML and Content Structure Affect SEO

- **Title Tags and Meta Descriptions**: The <title> tag tells search engines and users what the page is about. Similarly, meta descriptions summarize the page content for search engines, and while they don't directly affect rankings, they influence the click-through rate (CTR).

html

```
<title>Web Accessibility and SEO Best Practices</title>
<meta name="description" content="Learn best practices for improving web accessibility and SEO to create more inclusive and discoverable websites.">
```

- **Headings and Semantic HTML**: Proper use of <h1>, <h2>, <h3>, etc., tags helps structure content for both users and search engines. The <h1> tag should describe the main content of the page, followed by subheadings that organize the material.

html

```
<h1>Best Practices for Web Accessibility and SEO</h1>
<h2>What is Web Accessibility?</h2>
<h3>Why Accessibility Matters</h3>
```

- **Internal Linking**: Linking related pages within your site helps both users and search engines navigate the website. It improves the overall site structure and ensures that search engines can crawl all pages.

How Search Engines Crawl and Index Pages

Search engines use **web crawlers** to scan web pages, index the content, and rank it based on relevance and quality. The structure of your HTML, the use of keywords, and proper meta tags all contribute to how well your site performs in search rankings.

---

3. Best Practices for Accessibility

To ensure that your site is accessible, follow these best practices:

ARIA (Accessible Rich Internet Applications) Roles

ARIA roles help make dynamic content and advanced user interface elements accessible to screen readers. They provide information about the function of an element and its relationships with other elements. For example, if you have a dropdown menu, you can use ARIA roles to describe it for screen readers:

html

```
<div role="menu" aria-label="Main Navigation">
 <a href="#" role="menuitem">Home</a>
 <a href="#" role="menuitem">About</a>
</div>
```

Alt Text for Images

Every image on a webpage should include descriptive **alt text** that provides context for users who rely on screen readers. Alt text should be succinct but descriptive enough to convey the purpose of the image. If the image is purely decorative, an empty alt attribute (alt="") is appropriate:

html

```
<img src="logo.png" alt="Company logo">
```

Keyboard Navigation

Ensure that users can navigate your site using only a keyboard. This includes ensuring that all interactive elements (links, buttons, form fields, etc.) are focusable and accessible via the Tab key. Use the :focus CSS pseudo-class to style focusable elements:

css

```
a:focus, button:focus {
  outline: 2px solid #005fcc;
}
```

Color Contrast and Text Size

Ensure sufficient contrast between text and background colors to make the text legible for users with low vision or color blindness. You can use online tools like the **Contrast Checker** to verify that your text meets WCAG guidelines for color contrast.

Additionally, make sure text is resizable without loss of content or functionality. This can be achieved by using relative units like em, rem, and % instead of fixed pixel sizes.

Semantic HTML

Using semantic HTML tags like <header>, <footer>, <article>, and <section> improves accessibility by defining the structure of your content. These tags help screen readers and search engines understand the content's hierarchy and context.

For instance:

html

```
<header>
  <h1>Welcome to Our Website</h1>
  <nav>
   <ul>
    <li><a href="#">Home</a></li>
    <li><a href="#">About</a></li>
   </ul>
  </nav>
</header>
<main>
  <section>
   <h2>Our Services</h2>
   <p>We offer web development and design services.</p>
  </section>
</main>
<footer>
```

```
<p>&copy; 2024 Our Website. All rights reserved.</p>
</footer>
```

---

4. Real-World Example: Making a Simple Webpage Accessible and Improving SEO

Let's consider a basic webpage example where we will apply both accessibility improvements and SEO optimizations.

Original HTML Structure:

html

```
<!DOCTYPE html>
<html lang="en">
  <head>
    <meta charset="UTF-8">
    <meta name="viewport" content="width=device-width, initial-scale=1.0">
    <title>Simple Webpage</title>
  </head>
  <body>
    <h1>Welcome to Our Website</h1>
    <p>This website is about web development.</p>
    <img src="developer.jpg" alt="A web developer working on a computer">
    <a href="https://www.example.com">Click here to learn more</a>
  </body>
</html>
```

Optimized for Accessibility and SEO:

1. **Add semantic HTML**: Organize the content using appropriate HTML5 tags.

2. **Use ARIA roles**: Improve navigation and accessibility for dynamic content.

3. **Include alt text**: Ensure the image has a proper description.

4. **Use heading structure**: Properly structure the headings to aid both users and search engines.

5. **SEO Meta Tags**: Add meta descriptions and improve keyword relevance.

html

```
<!DOCTYPE html>
<html lang="en">
 <head>
  <meta charset="UTF-8">
  <meta name="viewport" content="width=device-width, initial-scale=1.0">
  <meta name="description" content="Learn about web development and best practices for accessibility and SEO.">
  <title>Web Development Basics - Accessible & SEO Friendly</title>
 </head>
 <body>
  <header>
   <h1>Welcome to Our Web Development Guide</h1>
   <nav role="navigation" aria-label="Main Navigation">
    <ul>
     <li><a href="#about">About Us</a></li>
     <li><a href="#contact">Contact</a></li>
    </ul>
```

```
    </nav>
  </header>

  <main>
    <section>
      <h2 id="about">About Us</h2>
      <p>We provide web development tutorials with a focus on accessibility
and SEO optimization.</p>
      <img src="developer.jpg" alt="A web developer working on a computer"
/>
    </section>

    <section>
      <h3>Learn More</h3>
      <p>Click below to get started with our comprehensive tutorials.</p>
      <a    href="https://www.example.com"    title="Learn    more    about    web
development" role="button">Learn More</a>
    </section>
  </main>

  <footer>
    <p>&copy; 2024 Web Development Guide. All rights reserved.</p>
  </footer>
  </body>
</html>
```

In this optimized version:

- **Semantic HTML** is used, with <header>, <main>, <section>, and <footer> tags.

- **SEO improvements** include adding a <meta name="description"> tag for better indexing.
- **ARIA roles** are applied to the navigation for screen reader users.
- **Alt text** is provided for the image to enhance accessibility.
- **Headings are structured** logically for both SEO and screen reader compatibility.

Web accessibility and SEO are critical components of front-end development. By applying best practices for accessibility, such as using semantic HTML, ARIA roles, proper alt text, and ensuring keyboard navigability, you ensure your site is inclusive and usable for all users. Similarly, optimizing your site for SEO by using proper heading structures, meta tags, and content organization helps improve its visibility in search engine results. Together, accessibility and SEO lead to a better, more user-friendly, and discoverable web experience.

CHAPTER 20: PUTTING IT ALL TOGETHER – BUILDING A COMPLETE FRONT-END PROJECT

After learning the fundamentals of **HTML**, **CSS**, and **JavaScript**, the next natural step is to apply your knowledge by creating a full front-end project. In this chapter, we'll go through the process of **planning**, **designing**, and **deploying** a complete website, using everything you've learned so far. This hands-on approach will help solidify your understanding and demonstrate how to turn your skills into a real-world project.

We'll end with a **real-world example** where you will build and deploy a **portfolio website**, showcasing all the front-end development concepts covered in the book.

---

1. Project Planning and Structure

Before diving into the code, a well-thought-out project plan is essential to ensure your website is organized and your development process runs smoothly. The planning phase helps you define the scope of your project, understand its requirements, and break down the tasks into manageable steps.

Steps for Planning a Front-End Project:

- **Define the Purpose and Goals**: Start by deciding what your website will do. Are you building a personal portfolio, a blog, an e-commerce site, or something else? Defining the purpose will guide all your design and development decisions.

  Example: A **personal portfolio** website to showcase your projects, skills, and experience.

- **Create Wireframes and Mockups**: Wireframes are simple sketches of the layout of your website, showing how elements will be structured. Mockups are more detailed, often designed using tools like Figma, Sketch, or Adobe XD, and represent how the website will look with actual colors, typography, and images.

  Example: For a portfolio website, you might have a **home page**, **about section**, **portfolio gallery**, and **contact form**.

- **Determine Technologies**: Decide which technologies you will use for the project. In our case, HTML, CSS, and JavaScript, but you may also consider additional tools like frameworks (e.g., React, Vue) or pre-processors (e.g., SASS).

- **Create a Development Roadmap**: Break down the project into smaller, manageable tasks (design, HTML structure, styling, JavaScript functionality, etc.), and set milestones or deadlines.

Project Example Plan: Portfolio Website

- **Home Page**: Introduction, skills, and a short bio.
- **Portfolio Section**: Grid layout of projects with images and descriptions.
- **About Page**: Personal background, education, and contact details.
- **Contact Form**: A simple form for users to reach out.

2. Designing with HTML, CSS, and JavaScript

Once you've planned the project and have a clear understanding of the structure, it's time to start coding. Here, we'll use everything we've learned about **HTML**, **CSS**, and **JavaScript** to bring the website to life.

Step-by-Step Process for Building the Portfolio Website:

1. **HTML Structure**: Start by laying out the structure of your webpage. Use semantic tags like <header>, <nav>, <main>, <section>, and <footer> to organize the content.

Example (Home Page HTML):

html

```
<header>
  <h1>John Doe's Portfolio</h1>
  <nav>
   <ul>
     <li><a href="#about">About</a></li>
     <li><a href="#portfolio">Portfolio</a></li>
     <li><a href="#contact">Contact</a></li>
   </ul>
  </nav>
</header>

<main>
  <section id="about">
   <h2>About Me</h2>
   <p>I'm a front-end developer with a passion for building beautiful
and functional websites.</p>
  </section>

  <section id="portfolio">
   <h2>My Work</h2>
   <div class="project-grid">
     <div class="project">
       <img src="project1.jpg" alt="Project 1">
       <h3>Project 1</h3>
       <p>Description of the project.</p>
     </div>
     <!-- More projects here -->
```

```
    </div>
  </section>

  <section id="contact">
   <h2>Contact Me</h2>
    <form id="contact-form">
     <input type="text" id="name" placeholder="Your Name" required>
     <input type="email" id="email" placeholder="Your Email"
required>
     <textarea    id="message"    placeholder="Your    Message"
required></textarea>
     <button type="submit">Send</button>
    </form>
  </section>
 </main>

<footer>
 <p>&copy; 2024 John Doe</p>
</footer>
```

2. **CSS Styling**: Apply styles to the layout using **CSS**. Use **Flexbox** or **CSS Grid** for responsive design and **media queries** for mobile responsiveness.

Example (Basic CSS):

css

```
body {
 font-family: Arial, sans-serif;
```

```css
  margin: 0;
  padding: 0;
  background-color: #f4f4f4;
}

header {
  background-color: #333;
  color: white;
  padding: 1em 0;
}

nav ul {
  list-style: none;
  padding: 0;
}

nav ul li {
  display: inline;
  margin: 0 15px;
}

nav ul li a {
  color: white;
  text-decoration: none;
}

.project-grid {
  display: grid;
  grid-template-columns: repeat(auto-fill, minmax(250px, 1fr));
  gap: 20px;
```

```css
}

.project img {
 width: 100%;
 height: auto;
}

/* Mobile responsive */
@media (max-width: 768px) {
 nav ul li {
   display: block;
   margin: 10px 0;
 }
}
```

3. **JavaScript Interactivity**: Add **JavaScript** to make the website interactive. For example, you can add an event listener to submit the contact form without reloading the page.

   Example (Basic JavaScript for Form Submission):

   javascript

```javascript
document.getElementById('contact-form').addEventListener('submit',
function(event) {
 event.preventDefault(); // Prevent default form submission
 alert('Form submitted!');
});
```

4. **Polish and Enhance**: Add final touches, such as hover effects, animations, and advanced form validation.

---

3. Deploying Your Website

Once you've built and tested your website locally, the next step is to deploy it to the web so others can access it. There are several hosting options, but for a simple static website (like our portfolio), **GitHub Pages** is a popular and easy-to-use option.

Using GitHub Pages:

1. **Create a GitHub Repository**: Go to GitHub, create a new repository, and push your local project files to it.

2. **Enable GitHub Pages**: In your repository, go to **Settings > GitHub Pages**. Choose the main branch and the root folder as the source.

3. **Visit Your Website**: Once enabled, GitHub Pages will provide a URL where your website is hosted (e.g., https://yourusername.github.io/repository-name).

Other Hosting Options:

- **Netlify**: Great for static sites with continuous deployment.
- **Vercel**: Perfect for front-end projects, especially if you're using React, Next.js, or similar frameworks.

- **Firebase Hosting**: Excellent for static and dynamic sites, with built-in SSL and custom domain support.

4. Real-World Example: Building and Deploying a Portfolio Website

Let's put everything together and build a **portfolio website**. You can follow the steps outlined above to structure the HTML, style it with CSS, and add JavaScript functionality for the contact form.

Step 1: Plan the Layout: Define the sections you want—about, portfolio, contact—and organize them using wireframes.

Step 2: Create the HTML Structure: Build the layout with appropriate HTML tags, ensuring semantic structure.

Step 3: Style the Website: Use CSS to make your website visually appealing, incorporating Flexbox for layout and media queries for responsiveness.

Step 4: Add Interactivity: Enhance the user experience by adding JavaScript functionalities, like form validation or a smooth scroll effect.

Step 5: Deploy the Site: Once the site is complete, use GitHub Pages or another hosting platform to deploy it.

Building a full front-end project is a powerful way to cement your understanding of **HTML, CSS**, and **JavaScript**. By following the steps in this chapter, you will gain hands-on experience in structuring, styling, and adding interactivity to a website. Deploying the project makes it live and accessible to the world, further validating the skills you've learned.

This project will not only serve as a great way to demonstrate your abilities but also act as a portfolio piece that showcases your capabilities to future employers or clients.

www.ingramcontent.com/pod-product-compliance
Lightning Source LLC
LaVergne TN
LVHW022341060326
832902LV00022B/4183